Effective Intervention with Adolescents Who Have Offended Sexually

TRANSLATING RESEARCH INTO PRACTICE

Effective Intervention with Adolescents Who Have Offended Sexually

TRANSLATING RESEARCH INTO PRACTICE

Sue Righthand
University of Maine

Brittany Baird
Royal Ottawa Health Care Group

Ineke Way
Western Michigan University

Michael C. Seto
University of Ottawa Institute of Mental Health Research

BRANDON, VERMONT

Copyright © 2014 by the Safer Society Press, Brandon, Vermont

First Edition

All rights reserved. No part of this book may be reproduced in any form or by any electronic or mechanical means, including information storage and retrieval systems, without permission in writing from the publisher, except by a reviewer who may quote brief passages.

Printed in the United States of America
10 9 8 7 6 5 4 3 2 1

Library of Congress Cataloging-in-Publication Data
Righthand, Sue.
  Effective intervention with adolescents who have offended sexually : translating research into practice / Sue Righthand, Brittany Baird, Ineke Way, Michael C. Seto. — First edition.
    pages   cm
Includes bibliographical references.
ISBN 978-1-940234-00-7
1. Teenage sex offenders — Rehabilitation. 2. Teenage sex offenders — Services for.
3. Sexual abuse — Prevention I. Title.
HV9067.S48R499 2014
362.76 — dc23   2014030107

The SaferSociety PRESS

P.O. Box 340
Brandon, Vermont 05733
www.safersociety.org
(802) 247-3132

Safer Society Press is a program of the Safer Society Foundation, a 501(c)3 nonprofit dedicated to the prevention and treatment of sexual abuse. For more information, visit our website at www.safersociety.org

Effective Intervention with Adolescents Who Have Offended Sexually:
Translating Research into Practice

$15 plus shipping and handling
Order #WP163

Contents

Introduction 1

CHAPTER 1:
INCREASING EFFECTIVE INTERVENTIONS 5
Explanations of Adolescent Sexual Offending 5
A Typology of Adolescent Offending 7

CHAPTER 2:
TREATMENT TARGETS—CRIMINOGENIC NEEDS 11
    Sexuality 12
    Social Bonds and Orientation 17
    General Self-Regulation 21
    Social Competence 25
    Socio-Ecological Factors 28

CHAPTER 3:
INCREASING POSITIVE TREATMENT
OUTCOMES—RESPONSIVITY 33
    Introduction 33
    Developmental Factors 34
    Motivation and Change 34
    Responsibility and Change 35
    Learning Styles and Cognitive Abilities 38
    Mental Health and Behavioral Health Challenges
        and Co-occurring Disorders 39
    Additional Considerations 41

CHAPTER 4:
ASSESSMENT—RISK AND NEEDS
ASSESSMENT MEASURES 43

Contents

CHAPTER 5:
EFFECTIVE INTERVENTIONS 47
    Introduction 47
    Meta-Analytic Reviews Focusing Primarily on Adults
        Who Offended Sexually 49
    Meta-Analytic Findings Focusing on Children with
        Sexual Behavior Problems... 50
    Meta-Analytic Findings Involving Adolescents
        with Illegal Sexual Behavior.. 51
    Promising Treatment Models 52
    Possible Barriers to Treatment 56
    Treatment Engagement and Completion 56
    Caregiver Engagement 58

CHAPTER 6: SUMMARY AND DISCUSSION 59
    Assessment.. 59
    Treatment 60
    Future Research 62

Appendix A:
    Criminongenic Treatment Targets: Summary Table 64

Appendix B:
    Treatment Targets for Adolescents with Illegal Sexual Behaviors:
    Information from The Safer Society 2009 Nationwide Survey 70

References 73

Introduction

Sexual abuse by adolescents is a serious problem. Adolescents commit as many as a quarter of sexual offenses known to law enforcement and are responsible for over a third of sexual offenses against minors (see Finkelhor, Ormrod, & Chaffin, 2009). Adolescents who have offended sexually are a heterogeneous population (Hunter, 2006, 2007; Seto & Lalumière, 2010). Thus, their treatment needs vary; no single approach to treatment is likely to be effective for every youth. Individualized and evidence-based assessment and treatment are essential.

The main goal of this book is to summarize research to highlight dynamic risk factors that are important treatment targets when working with adolescents who have engaged in illegal sexual behavior (AISB). Adolescent behavior is influenced not only by individual factors but also interrelated systems that surround and interact with the youth, including his or her family, friends, school, workplace, neighborhood, and society. As a result, our conceptualization of dynamic risk factors includes these other systems as well, consistent with socio-ecological theories of child and human development (e.g., Bronfenbrenner, 1979). We focus in particular on family and peer factors, as these are more amenable to intervention by individual clinicians than community or sociocultural factors.

Our approach to understanding dynamic risk and protective factors in AISB is similar to Belsky's (1980) model of risk factors associated with child maltreatment and with the multisystemic framework offered by Henggeler and his colleagues (Henggeler, Schoenwald, Boruin, Rowland, & Cunningham, 1998) and validated for intervening with juvenile delinquency (Curtis, Ronan, & Borduin, 2004). Factors that influence sexual reoffending by AISB, by either increasing the likelihood of reoffending (risk factors) or mitigating the risk (protective factors), include individual (ontogenic) factors, family (micro-systemic) factors, community (exo-systemic) factors, and cultural (macro-systemic) factors. To be most effective, interventions at each of these levels may be required. Examples of relevant risk factors include—but are not limited to—individual factors such as "deviant" or atypical sexual interests, antisocial orientation, attitudes and beliefs that are supportive of sexual offending, social isolation, problematic intimate relationships, and not being engaged in or completing appropriate treatment; family factors such as problematic parent[1]–adolescent relationships and poor supervision and monitoring, as well as social influences such as negative peer influences and insufficient community and cultural supports.

Protective factors have received limited research with AISB (Spice, Viljoen, Latzman, Scalora, & Ullman, 2013), and only a few have received empirical support with this group of adolescents. No particular risk or protective factor is determinative. In general, the more risk factors that are present and the fewer strengths and protective factors available, the greater the risk of sexual or nonsexual reoffending. Risk and protective factors will be discussed in more detail later and are summarized in the Criminogenic Treatment Targets: Summary Table found in appendix A.

Last, as we will discuss in further detail below, adolescents vary greatly in the extent to which they need specialized sexual-behavior interventions. Because of their diversity, the kinds of interventions that are required to reduce their risk of reoffending and promote healthy, prosocial development also can vary.

We begin by describing a number of contemporary models of adolescent sexual offending, and by highlighting potential treatment targets. We then review promising or empirically supported treatment approaches for AISB and the research on treatment effectiveness. We conclude with a summary of our recommendations. Because most studies have focused on male adolescents, and females represent only a small minority of adolescents identified with sex-offending behaviors, this book will reflect research only on boys unless otherwise noted. When relevant, research pertaining to adults who offend sexually and adolescents who commit nonsexual offenses is discussed.

AISB have one consistent thing in common with each other: they have engaged in illegal sexual behavior. Otherwise, they can differ in myriad ways, including their motivations for offending, offense characteristics, victim characteristics, criminal history, developmental history, risk to reoffend, and treatment needs. For example, a subset of these youths are especially sexually

---

1 We will use the term *parent* to refer any adult in a parental, caretaking, and guardianship role.

aroused by children, whereas most are more likely to be opportunistic or situational in their offending (Seto, Lalumière, & Blanchard, 2000). Some AISB abuse significantly younger children, others offend against peers or adults, while a small subgroup abuse people of different age categories. Similarly, some AISB exhibit gender preferences in their offending, while others do not.

Their abusive behaviors also vary from noncontact behaviors such as exhibitionism or accessing child pornography to fondling, to forcible rape. Whereas some of these adolescents have committed only sexual offenses, many have committed nonsexual offenses as well as sexual offenses. In addition, some of these adolescents have experienced sexual abuse or other maltreatment as well as frequent changes in caregivers, some have shown serious conduct problems as children, but some have apparently developed without significant difficulties and with no known problems of a serious nature prior to their sexually abusive behavior. The likelihood that an adolescent will reoffend sexually or nonsexually varies greatly and depends on a variety of risk and protective factors.

In this review, we are primarily concerned with sexual offenses committed against prepubescent or pubescent children who are chronologically or developmentally significantly younger than the AISB, and with sexual offenses involving sexual coercion or violence toward peers or adults. We will not discuss statutory sexual crimes involving an adolescent who has what both parties consider to be consensual sex, with a younger youth below the legally mandated age of consent, or when both youths are below the age of consent but they are within three years of each other's ages and both consider themselves to be engaged in consensual sexual activities. Additionally, we also will not address child pornography offending and "sexting" images of underage youths.

1 Increasing Effective Interventions

As described above, AISB are heterogeneous. Due to this heterogeneity, the effectiveness of interventions can be increased when we understand explanatory models of sex offending, attend to relevant similarities and differences, and tailor interventions to meet individual needs and learning styles (Andrews & Bonta, 2010; Hanson, Bourgon, Helmus, & Hodgson, 2009).

Explanations of Adolescent Sexual Offending

Explanatory models are important because they provide a theoretical framework for risk assessment, assessment of treatment needs, and treatment delivery. A very important first consideration is whether AISB require their own explanatory models, as opposed to the well-established models of juvenile delinquency that have been developed over the past century (Quinsey, Skilling, Lalumière, & Craig, 2004). Some researchers have suggested that nonsexual conduct problems appear so frequently among these teens that sexual offending may be just one facet of an overall pattern of delinquent behavior (Milloy, 1994). Way and Urbaniak (2008) found that about half of AISB who are adjudicated for criminal sexual conduct have committed at least one nonsexual offense prior to their sexual offense. Similarly, France and Hudson (1993) reviewed studies and concluded that a majority of adolescents who commit sexual offenses have also committed nonsexual crimes, and approximately half would meet the diagnostic criteria for conduct disorder, which describes a pervasive and versatile pattern of antisocial behavior during childhood. If they reoffend, AISB are more likely to commit a new nonsexual crime than a sexual offense. Additionally, some studies suggest risk factors associated with general delinquency and violence among adolescents also increase the risk of sexual recidivism (e.g., Caldwell & Dickenson, 2009; McCann & Lussier, 2008; Parks & Bard, 2006; Nisbet, Wilson, & Smallbone, 2004; Waite, Keller, McGarvey, Wieckowski, Pinkerton, & Brown, 2005; Worling, Bookalam, & Litteljohn, 2012).

At the same time, most explanatory models are sex-offense-specific, and there are reasons to expect that AISB may differ in meaningful ways from their nonsexually offending peers and require specialized interventions. For example, Milloy (1994) reported that AISB tend to have less extensive criminal histories and substance use than adolescents who engage in nonsexual offenses, and Smith and Monastersky (1986) found that AISB with less previous contact with juvenile justice system were less likely to reoffend. Further, in their literature review on specialized assessment and treatment, Fanniff and Becker (2006) concluded that—despite limited research and methodological challenges—available findings suggested juvenile sex-offense-specific treatments that employed cognitive-behavioral interventions targeting sex-offense-specific attitudes and interests are "promising," as are multisystemic interventions.

To test the generalist and specialist perspectives, Seto and Lalumière (2010) conducted a meta-analysis of 59 studies comparing AISB with adolescents who had committed other kinds of offenses on theoretically relevant variables, including conduct-problem history, criminal history, antisocial traits, family problems, maltreatment, interpersonal difficulties, psychopathology, and sexual interests. If the generalist view is correct, then adolescents with sex offenses and those who appear only to engage in non-sex offenses should not differ on these variables; if the specialist view is correct, then the two groups should significantly differ. A mixed pattern suggests both views are partially correct, with the domains that distinguish the two groups of adolescents being the most relevant when intervening with a specific adolescent.

The Seto and Lalumière (2010) meta-analysis results suggested that AISB, on average, are less antisocial and have committed fewer criminal offenses than those who commit other types of offenses. AISB were more likely to have experienced sexual abuse or exposure to sexual violence in the family, had been exposed to pornography or sex earlier, and were more likely to have atypical sexual interests (e.g., reporting atypical sexual fantasies such as sexual attraction to prepubescent children). AISB were also more socially isolated, anxious, and lower in self-esteem. At the same time, AISB are a heterogeneous group. Way and Urbaniak (2008) cautioned against analyzing AISB as a homogeneous population, as AISB with and without other delinquent histories differ significantly from each other on a number of characteristics. Thus, a specialist–generalist dichotomy may not fully capture the diversity of AISB or the reasons they committed their sexual offenses.

A Typology of Adolescent Offending

Although there is no agreed-upon typological or classification system for AISB, a potentially useful model for conceptualizing the risk and needs of these adolescents is based upon early theories (Becker & Kaplan, 1988; O'Brien and Bera, 1986) and more recent empirical findings (e.g., Hunter, 2006, 2008; Hunter, Figueredo, Malamuth, & Becker, 2004; Way & Urbaniak, 2008). Hunter (2006, 2008) has reported findings from over a decade of AISB typology research he and his colleagues pursued. They identified five types of AISB: (1) life-course persistent antisocial type; (2) adolescent-onset "experimenter"; (3) socially impaired—anxious and depressed; (4) antisocial with pedophilic interests; and (5) non-antisocial with pedophilic interests. Hunter noted the first two types are consistent with Moffit's (1993) work regarding early onset persistent and adolescent onset–limited delinquency. Additionally, he reported that sex offending by adolescent onset "experimenters" and socially impaired AISB are likely to be transitory, especially when appropriate interventions are provided. Hunter (2006, 2008) observed the categories are not absolute and that youth may vary in severity. Attention to this diversity among AISB can facilitate effective interventions, placement in appropriate settings, and improve legal decision making.

Building on Hunter and his colleagues' work, we have combined the two groups for whom offending is most likely to be transitory and propose four groupings that can be used as a model when triaging AISB to appropriate services: (1) *situational*; (2) *early onset or serious delinquency*; (3) *atypical sexual interests/preoccupation*; and (4) *both serious delinquency and atypical sexual interests*. These four groups cross the two major risk dimensions identified in the sexual-offending literature, one having to do with *antisocial propensities* and the other having to do with *atypical sexual interests* (Hanson & Bussiere, 1998; Hanson & Morton-Bourgon, 2005). Adolescents who have few risk factors on the atypical sexual interests and early onset or serious delinquency dimensions are very likely to be situational in their offending and are the least likely to reoffend. AISB who are high in antisocial tendencies but low in atypical sexual interests generally have early onset or serious delinquency patterns of offending and are much more likely to reoffend nonsexually, rather than sexually. Those who are low in antisocial tendencies but high in atypical sexual interests are in the third group and are relatively more likely to commit a sexual offense if they reoffend. Lastly, the fourth group includes those who have many risk factors from both risk dimensions and, consequently, pose the greatest risk for both sexual and nonsexual reoffending.

Situational. Situational AISB have few risk factors associated with sexual and nonsexual offending. They may engage in minor delinquency, like many adolescents, but are low in antisocial tendencies and low in atypical sexual interests. They may not require treatment at all, or if they do require treatment, their intervention needs are limited, and treatment duration is usually brief. Offenses might be a result of increased sex drive following the onset of puberty, curiosity, limited awareness of how to manage sexual impulses, and opportunity (e.g., access to a younger sibling), perhaps coupled with a poor understanding of healthy sexual relationships or wrongfulness of their sexual misconduct. Some of these adolescents may be reacting to their own childhood sexual abuse or early exposure to sex or sexual violence. Others may be lonely and socially isolated, with few sexual or romantic prospects.

Early onset or serious delinquency. The sexually abusive behavior of adolescents who have early onset or serious delinquency is typically opportunistic and more likely to occur in the context of other antisocial or delinquent behavior, for example, while consuming alcohol or drugs, or by sexually assaulting a woman as part of a home robbery. Their sexual interests and urges are age-appropriate, but they may have coercive or forced sex with older children or use peers or adults to fulfill their sexual needs, disregarding the potential consequences for themselves and others. Established treatments for juvenile delinquency are the most appropriate for this group.

Persistent atypical sexual interests/preoccupation. This third group appears to be relatively small in number (Clift, Rajcik, & Gretton, 2009; Driemeyer, Yoon, & Briken, 2011; Hunter & Becker, 1994; Seto, Murphy, Page, & Ennis, 2003; Seto, 2008, 2013), but this group presents with specialized treatment needs because of excessive sexual preoccupation, sexual attraction to children, and/or sexual interest in sexual coercion or violence. For example, Seto et al. (2000) studied AISB with child victims and found that 7 percent of those with girl victims and 21 percent of those with boy victims showed equal or greater sexual arousal to children than to adolescents or adults when assessed in the laboratory. Such individuals may be unlikely to have notable histories of conduct problems or nonsexual offending, but their persistent atypical sexual interests and behavior are risk factors for further sexually abusive behavior (Clift et al., 2009).

Serious delinquency and atypical sexual interests. A fourth group of AISB—individuals with both serious delinquency and atypical sexual interests—are expected to be the most likely to sexually reoffend. This premise is consistent with adult sexual recidivism research (e.g., Hanson & Bourgon, 2005; Seto, Harris, Rice, & Barbaree, 2004). Psychopathy, especially when associated with atypical sexual arousal, has been associated with persistent sexual offending among adults (e.g., Quinsey, Rice, & Harris, 1995; Seto & Barbaree, 1999). Although the combination of serious delinquency or psychopathy *and* atypical sexual interests has not been a specific focus in recent studies of AISB, Gretton, McBride, Hare, O'Shaughnessy, and Kuma (2001) found elevated psychopathy and penile plethysmography (PPG) scores were associated with higher rates of general recidivism. More recently, Clift et al. (2009) found higher PPG scores at discharge were associated with greater sexual recidivism, and serious delinquency and psychopathy scores also have been associated with sexual reoffending (e.g., Caldwell, Ziemke, & Vitacco, 2008). Thus, the combination of serious delinquency or psychopathic traits in AISB and atypical sexual arousal may be an especially risky combination for sexual and nonsexual reoffending.

RISK, NEED, AND RESPONSIVITY PRINCIPLES

The risk-need-responsivity (RNR) model has been discussed in the criminal justice literature for decades (see Andrews & Bonta, 2010). This model describes three major principles of correctional rehabilitation and human service delivery that, if met, are associated with greater reductions in criminal recidivism among both adults (Andrews & Bonta) and juveniles (e.g., Pealer & Latessa, 2004), including adults and juveniles who have committed sexual offenses (Hanson, Bourgon, Helmus, & Hodgson, 2009). The *risk principle* asserts that intervention intensity should be matched to risk level, such that individuals with the most risks associated with recidivism receive the most intense treatment, whereas individuals with few risk factors might receive basic supervision and limited treatment, or none at all. The *need principle* states that interventions are most effective when they target "criminogenic needs" (i.e., dynamic risk factors, defined below). The *responsivity principle* purports that interventions that are tailored to individual learning style are more effective. For most people involved in the criminal or juvenile justice system, interventions that are cognitive-behavioral in orientation, focused on pro-social skill development, and are pragmatic, are the most suitable under the RNR model. We begin this by reviewing criminogenic needs in the next chapter and then discuss responsivity factors.

2 Treatment Targets—Criminogenic Needs

Research findings from studies of risk factors associated with sexual reoffending by AISB are relatively limited in number; often have methodological problems, such as small sample sizes, convenience samples, or diverse outcome measures; and often have inconsistent results. In spite of these challenges, some consistent patterns have emerged. Findings from two meta-analyses of sexual and nonsexual recidivism in AISB (Heilbrun, Lee, & Cottle, 2005; McCann & Lussier, 2008), along with two meta-analyses that included both adolescents and adults who had committed sexually abusive behaviors (Helmus, Hanson, Babchishin, & Mann, 2013; Hanson & Morton-Bourgon, 2005), help identify relevant treatment targets. Only a couple of studies have specifically investigated factors that might protect and reduce the likelihood of sexual reoffending by these youths, and in at least one of these studies, none of the items was significant (e.g., Spice et al., 2013). The limited research pertaining to desistance from offending is also evident by the few studies that have reported characteristics of the adolescents who appeared to stop engaging in illegal sexual behaviors (e.g., Smith & Monastersky, 1986).

Some factors associated with recidivism are static, such as historical events that cannot be changed; others are dynamic factors (defined as *criminogenic needs* by Andrews, Bonta, & Hoge, 1990) and, theoretically, can be changed by intervention and time. Assessments that include risk-assessment measures that identify dynamic risk factors can be very helpful for identifying how to intervene (Viljoen et al., 2012).

Individually focused treatment needs to include personal characteristics, attitudes, traits, skills, and behaviors. They may be risk factors that require amelioration, or strengths and protective factors that need to be maintained or enhanced. The domains that follow include the general categories of *sexuality* (e.g., atypical interests and sex drive/preoccupation); *social bonds and orientation* (e.g., pro- and antisocial orientations); *self-regulation* (e.g., emotional and impulse management); and *social competence* (e.g., social isolation, emotional congruence with young children, conflicts in intimate relationships, negative peer associations).

Sexuality

In this section, we discuss the roles that sexuality factors can play, including normative sexual development, high sex drive/preoccupation, sexual self-regulation problems, and atypical sexual interests.

Normative sexual development. The neurobiological changes associated with puberty occur as early as 9 to 10 years of age (e.g., Hyde & DeLamater, 1997). Feelings of sexual attraction may first occur between 10 and 12 years, with the onset of sexual fantasies developing several months to a year later (Herman-Giddens et al., 2001). Sex-hormone levels increase dramatically with puberty, accompanied by an increase in sexual thoughts and feelings. Moreover, puberty and then adolescence is a time of rapid brain development, extending into early adulthood. This developmental stage is characterized by risk taking, impulsivity, excessive self-focus, poor judgment, and limited regard to the future consequences of one's behavior, as well as strong feelings of sexual arousal and urges. During this developmental period, "atypical" sexual interests and behaviors may be fluid, exploratory, and opportunistic.

Atypical sexual interests. Atypical sexual interests, sexual arousal, and sexual behavior are, by definition, uncommon and unusual. Not all atypical sexual interests or behaviors are abusive or illegal (Barbaree & Marshall, 2006). For example, paraphilias (atypical sexual interests) that involve nonhuman objects (such as shoe fetishism) or anomalous sexual behaviors between consenting age-appropriate partners (such as bondage and submission) are atypical, but they are not abusive or illegal unless they involve persons who cannot, or who do not, consent.

Research studies of sexual interests, arousal patterns, and behavior in adolescents are limited in number. A significant methodological challenge involves discomfort or prohibitions for asking adolescents questions about their sexual interests and behaviors, especially non-offending adolescents. Thus, accurate information about details such as masturbation frequency or the content of sexual fantasies is lacking. Given the absence of specific information about normative sexual thoughts and behaviors among adolescents, it is not surprising that accurate information about the frequency of atypical sexual arousal involving children or coercive sex is unknown. The available research with adults and adolescents suggests that a persistent atypical interest involving prepubescent children is rare in the general population, estimated as 3 percent or less (cf. Seto, 2008, 2013). Studies (e.g., Hunter and Becker, 1994) have found the incidence of atypical sexual arousal may be more of a problem for adolescents who sexually offend against young children, particularly those who offend against boys. When present, persistent atypical sexual interests are an important treatment target. For example, in a study of adults who have offended sexually, Kingston, Federoff, Firestone, Curry, and Bradford (2008) found that viewing pornography depicting children or violence was associated with increased sexual reoffending.

Zakireh, Ronis, and Knight (2008) compared AISB in residential versus outpatient treatment, as well as adolescents in the same settings who had committed nonsexual offenses. They found that AISB in residential placements reported significantly more atypical sexual interests and behaviors than the other groups of teens. Although not a recidivism study, adolescents placed in residential settings are perceived by legal and clinical decision makers to pose a greater risk to community safety than those treated in the community, and in other research they have been found to have more risk factors and clinical needs than adolescents treated in the community (e.g., Righthand et al., 2005).

McCann and Lussier's (2008) meta-analytic study, and narrative literature reviews of sexual recidivism rates among AISB (e.g., Worling & Långström, 2003) also indicate that atypical sexual interests, if present, require intervention. Included in these reviews are studies (e.g., Kahn & Chambers, 1991; Schram et al., 1991; Worling & Curren, 2000) that have found atypical sexual interests to be related to increased rates of sexual reoffending or a greater number of sexual victims (Kenny, Keogh, & Seidler, 2001). These studies, however, relied on self-report and clinical judgments to determine the existence of atypical sexual interests, rather than more objective measures such as visual reaction time or phallometric assessments (e.g., Abel et al., 2004). More recently, Clift et al. (2009) found that posttreatment phallometrically assessed sexual arousal to male or female children was significantly associated with sexual recidivism. These findings add further support indicating that, when present, atypical sexual interests are important treatment targets.

Sex drive and preoccupation. Sexual behaviors are expressions of sexual interests, arousal, and drive. When someone offends sexually, this behavior may be a coercive expression of normative sexual interests, an expression of excessive sex drive or sexual preoccupation, and/or an expression of atypical sexual interests. Sexual offending is unlikely, however, to be an expression of sexual naïveté or ignorance. AISB often have had previous consenting sexual experiences (Ryan, Miyoshi, Metzner, Krugman, & Fryer, 1996). Other research has shown that their experiences are on par with those of adolescents who have offended with nonsexual offenses (Seto & Lalumière, 2010), or exceeded the experiences of comparison groups of adolescents who have not engaged in sexual offenses (McCord, McCord, & Venden, 1962, as cited in Knight & Prentky, 1993). Thus, psycho-education to increase basic knowledge about sexuality topics is usually not a criminogenic treatment target among AISB. As we discuss later, however, some AISB can benefit from education about developing and maintaining suitable sexual relationships, negotiating sexual consent, correcting erroneous attitudes and beliefs that excuse sexual offending, and effectively managing their sexual thoughts, fantasies, or urges.

The relationship between sexual preoccupation and sexual recidivism among adolescents has received limited research attention. In their 2005 meta-analysis, Hanson and Morton-Bourgon found a significant association between sexual preoccupation and sexual recidivism and described it as a "promising" dynamic risk factor (p. 1158). They examined studies of AISB in their set of mostly adult samples and noted, overall, the effect sizes for risk factors were similar for the adolescents and adults, but this does not necessarily mean sexual preoccupation plays a similar role for AISB as it does for adults who offend sexually.

In a recent study, however, Worling et al. (2012) found obsessive sexual interests/preoccupation with sexual thoughts was significantly correlated with sexual reoffending. Also, in their meta-analysis of nine AISB recidivism studies, Heilbrun et al. (2005) found that noncontact sexual offenses were related to repeat sexual offending. It is possible that noncontact sexual offending (e.g., exposing one's genitals to unsuspecting strangers, or intentionally viewing an unsuspecting person while he or she undresses or bathes or otherwise engages in an intimate, private act) reflects excessive sexual preoccupation as well as atypical sexual interests.

Parks and Bard (2006) found that a subgroup of adolescents with both child, and peer or older-aged, victims had higher ratings for sex drive and preoccupation compared with adolescents who only abused children, or those who only abused peer-aged or older victims. Although Parks and Bard did not find this group to have higher sexual recidivism rates than the others, recent meta-analytic findings showed higher ratings of sex drive and preoccupation are associated with higher rates of sexual recidivism (Viljoen et al., 2012).

Research suggests that excessive sexual preoccupation and sex drive are infrequent among adolescents (Zakireh, Ronis, & Knight, 2008). Zakireh and colleagues found, however, that adolescents who had offended sexually and who were in residential treatment reported significantly higher rates of sexual preoccupation, compulsivity, and drive than adolescents with sex-offense histories who received outpatient treatment. Importantly, their rates also were higher than adolescents with nonsexual offenses who were treated in residential or outpatient settings, suggesting that a lack of access to sexual partners while in residential settings cannot fully explain this difference.

Although studies focusing on the frequency of pornography use and sexual reoffending by adolescents are needed, frequent pornography use may signal sexual preoccupation and, thus, may be a relevant treatment target. In a study of adults with sex offenses, Kingston et al. (2008) found frequent pornography viewing was associated with sexual reoffending by adults considered at high risk of sexual reoffending due to other risk factors, but not by those at lower risk levels. A salient issue for adolescents is the increasingly young age of exposure to hardcore and atypical pornography content as a result of increased availability via the Internet (e.g., Sabina, Wolak, & Finkelhor, 2008).

Sexual self-regulation. Although immature, impulsive, and poorly thought-out behaviors are not uncommon or necessarily abnormal among adolescents, sexual self-regulation skills can be relevant treatment targets for adolescents who offend sexually. Learning to manage sexual arousal and satisfy sexual urges in healthy, nonabusive, and satisfying ways can be an important treatment target.

Even in the absence of atypical sexual interests or sexual preoccupation, adolescents must manage their normative sexual urges and impulses appropriately and legally, without harming others or themselves. Smith and Monastersky (1986) found that AISB in their sample tended to have "unhealthy" attitudes about sex, defined by the authors as "a naïve assertion... that any sexual behavior is abnormal and to be avoided" (p. 123). For adolescents whose offending is situational or opportunistic, getting caught may be a sufficient deterrent from reoffending; others may require relatively brief interventions to facilitate appropriate sexual self-regulation (e.g., learning the laws, the reasons for them, and the consequences for violating them; fully understanding what consent is and how to ensure it; and learning to manage one's sexual arousal and urges legally and how to get one's sexual needs met safely either through masturbation that does not reinforce interest in illegal images or fantasies, or through consensual and legal sexual activity).

Attitudes and beliefs regarding sex and sex offending. Multiple research studies with college students have demonstrated a relationship between attitudes and beliefs that support or condone impersonal sex and sexually aggressive behavior. In particular, Malamuth and his colleagues have demonstrated that attitudes and beliefs that they labeled "hostile masculinity" (negative, stereotypical views about women and sex) explain sexual aggression committed by young college men, and can predict sexual aggression after 10 years of follow-up (Malamuth, Linz, Heavey, Barnes, & Acker, 1995; Vega & Malamuth, 2007).

Although research with adolescents is more limited, some youths develop an impersonal or casual approach to sex as well as hostility toward women. In a large survey of 1,600 AISB (Ryan et al., 1996), about one-third perceived sex as a way to demonstrate love or caring for another person; others considered sex as a way to feel power and control, to dissipate anger, or to hurt, degrade, or punish. Therapist-identified "thinking errors" during treatment (Schram et al., 1991), such as blaming the victim (Kahn & Chambers, 1991), have been associated with increased rates of sexual reoffending among adolescents, and adolescents who desisted in offending were less likely than their counterparts to blame their victim for the sexual offense. Kenny et al. (2001) found that maladaptive cognitions (e.g., "she smiled at me so that meant she wanted to have sex") were related to increased deviant sexual fantasies, and more deviant sexual fantasies were associated with having had a greater numbers of victims. Other attitudes that may support sexual offending include the belief that young children want to have or have the capacity to consent to sex and benefit from sex with much older people.

Additionally, two meta-analytic studies also provide some support for addressing attitudes supportive of sexual offending. Hanson and Morton-Bourgon's (2005) meta-analytic findings revealed a small but positive association between attitudes supportive of sexual offending and recidivism. As noted previously, their quantitative review included primarily adult studies, but they also examined 15 studies of adolescents and noted the effect sizes for the adolescents were similar to those for adults. Similarly, a more recent meta-analysis also found a small but positive association between attitudes and beliefs supporting sexually abusive behavior and sexual recidivism (Helmus et al., 2013). Approximately a third of their samples involved adolescents.

Of further concern are Malamuth and Brown's (1994) research findings from their study of adults regarding how maladaptive attitudes and beliefs about sexual roles and behavior can affect interpersonal relationships and sexual behavior. These researchers found that men with negative, unhealthy beliefs about women and sex were more likely to misinterpret social cues in videotaped vignettes and presumably may also be more likely to misinterpret cues during real-life social encounters. Furthermore, Knight, Ronis, and Zakireh (2009) found greater hostility toward women among AISB who continued sex offending into adulthood.

Not all AISB espouse attitudes and beliefs that justify or support sexual offending. Some may perpetrate sexual abuse impulsively, without thinking about right or wrong; and other adolescents may not fully appreciate the wrongfulness of the sexually abusive behavior. When attitudes and beliefs supportive of offending influence how an adolescent perceives his or her world, however, such attitudes require intervention, not just because they constitute a criminogenic need, but because resolving such attitudes may facilitate healthier and more rewarding intimate relationships. (See the "Sexuality" subsection in appendix A: Criminogenic Treatment Targets: Summary Table).

Social Bonds and Orientation

In this section, we review antisocial orientation and antisocial attitudes and beliefs, and discuss the importance of facilitating pro-social bonds and orientations that include attitudes and values *in*consistent with sexual and nonsexual offending.

Antisocial orientation. Hanson and Morton-Bourgon (2005) asserted that an "antisocial orientation facilitates sexual offending because individuals will not commit sexual crimes unless they are (*a*) willing to hurt others, (*b*) can convince themselves that they are not harming their victims, or (*c*) feel unable to stop themselves" (p. 1154). When defining antisocial orientation, they referred to antisocial personality traits such as impulsivity or callousness, lifestyle instability, and a history of rule violations. Rapists are more likely than those who sexually abuse children to have an antisocial orientation, but factors such as hostility and lifestyle instability are associated with sexual recidivism in both groups. Other studies have found similar findings with AISB (e.g., Knight & Sims-Knight, 2004). Van der Put, van Vugt, Stams, Deković, and van der Laan (2013) found AISB with peer-aged or adult victims had more substantial criminal histories, conduct problems, antisocial attitudes and beliefs, delinquent peer associations, and substance abuse than those who targeted children.

Research findings pertaining to the relationship between an antisocial orientation and sexual recidivism among AISB have increasing research support. For example, Worling and Långström (2003) concluded that empirical support demonstrating an association between antisocial orientation and sexual recidivism was lacking. More recently, in a long-term follow-up study of AISB, Worling et al. (2012) found that an antisocial orientation was associated with sexual reoffending. Whether or not someone has an antisocial orientation may be very relevant for persistent sexual and/or nonsexual offending. Schram et al. (1991) found that AISB who desisted from future offending were less likely to have "sociopathic" tendencies and were less likely to have been previously convicted of any kind of violent or nonviolent crime.

Hanson and Morton-Bourgon's (2005) meta-analysis indicated the major predictors of sexual recidivism for AISB were the same as for adults who reoffended sexually: sexual deviance and an antisocial orientation. An antisocial orientation also was strongly associated with nonsexual violent and general offending. McCann and Lussier (2008) conducted a meta-analysis of 18 studies of AISB. Similar to Hanson and Morton-Bourgon, they found sexual deviance and a domain they called "antisociality" were statistically significant in their association with sexual recidivism, but the effect sizes were smaller. McCann and Lussier pointed out that the studies included in their analyses did not operationalize sexual deviance and antisocial orientation as dynamic factors that may resolve with ongoing adolescent development.

Rajilic and Gretton (2010) found that most of the adolescents in their sample who had no histories of nonsexual offending did not commit a new sexual or nonsexual offense. They found that antisociality indicators were predictive of sexual reoffending among the adolescents in the sex-offense-only group. Diagnoses of conduct disorder (CD) and oppositional defiant disorder (ODD) also have been associated with sexual reoffending by AISB (Epperson, Ralston, Flowers, & Dewitt, 2006). It may be that some AISB with antisocial orientations have had early onset conduct problems and, as described in Moffitt's (1993) developmental taxonomy, belong to a smaller group of youths who begin delinquency in childhood, continue through adolescence, and persist into adulthood, in contrast with the majority of youths who begin offending in their early to mid-teens and desist by the end of adolescence.

Although only a minority of adolescents who engage in delinquency or sexual offending present with substantial psychopathic traits (e.g., Gretton et al., 2001), research studies have found that callous and unemotional traits are associated with the development of sexual offending (Daversa & Knight, 2007; Knight & Sims-Knight, 2003) and increased violence during sexual offending (Knight & Guay, 2006). In addition, Caldwell et al. (2008) found that very high Psychopathy Checklist: Youth Version scores (PCL: YV; Forth, Kosson, & Hare, 2003) were significantly associated with sexual, violent, and nonsexual recidivism. (The Psychopathy Checklist: Youth Version is a well-validated, evaluator-rated measure of psychopathic traits among adolescents.) Fortunately, further studies suggest that adolescents who are diagnosed with CD or ODD, and even those who have psychopathic traits, can respond positively to evidence-based interventions (e.g., Caldwell et al., 2007; Henggeler, Melton, Brondino, Scherer, & Hanley, 1997; Sawyer & Borduin, 2011). More generally, meta-analytic findings provide very good support for the effectiveness of therapeutic interventions with youths who commit a wide range of offenses (Lipsey, 2009). Adolescents with an antisocial orientation and those who are rule violators, however, are most likely to be noncompliant with treatment and drop out or be terminated from treatment prematurely (Hunter & Figueredo, 1999).

Antisocial attitudes and beliefs. Just as not all AISB have attitudes and beliefs supportive of sexual offending, not all adolescents who break laws have habitual ways of thinking that encourage, rationalize, and support criminal and violent behavior. Such criminal thinking involves values that are self-centered, disregard the welfare of others, and view dishonesty, crime, and violence as justifiable and appropriate options. Because of their sense of entitlement, youths who endorse antisocial attitudes and beliefs may believe that they are above the law; that the rules and conventions of society do not apply to them or their compatriots, and value rebelling against norms. When people hold antisocial attitudes and beliefs, they may ridicule, resent, and defy societal rules and authority at home, in school, and in the community. They may be hostile to authority figures and may be oppositional or noncompliant with probation conditions and treatment requirements. Not surprisingly, pro-criminal sentiments are strong risk factors for violent reoffending, including sexual recidivism (e.g., Hawkins et al., 2000).

Seto and Lalumière's (2010) meta-analytic review comparing AISB with those who had committed nonsexual crimes found no significant differences between the two groups on measures of antisocial attitudes and beliefs. Antisocial attitudes and beliefs may be transitory or entrenched, as when an adolescent adheres to an antisocial orientation and lifestyle. When present, interventions that address such attitudes and beliefs may help facilitate pro-social thinking and lifestyles that are incompatible with reoffending. The importance of this domain is further highlighted by the Surgeon General's report on *Youth Violence* and its finding that having an intolerant attitude regarding criminal behavior was the only individual factor that protected against violence (Department of Health and Human Services, 2001).

Peer associations. Hawkins et al. (2000) found "weak social ties" increase the risk of violent behavior. They defined "weak social ties" as isolation from pro-social peers, including being unpopular with, or rejected by, peers. They suggested it was not social isolation itself that increased risk, but the delinquent or negative peers an adolescent might associate with in the absence of pro-social ties. Meta-analytic findings regarding youth violence, serious delinquency, and general juvenile recidivism have shown that negative and delinquent peer association is a strong predictor for both the development and persistence of general offending (Cottle, Lee, & Heilbun, 2001; Hawkins et al., 2000; Lipsey & Derzon, 1998). Few studies have found negative peer associations to be related to juvenile sexual reoffending, however.

In a confidential survey involving a large study of incarcerated adolescents, 11 percent of the males acknowledge a history of forcing someone to have sex (Morris, Anderson, & Knox, 2002). Knowing a person who had offended sexually was associated with greater self-reported sexual violence, suggesting peer influences on sexual offending. Ageton (1983) also found that juveniles who admitted to engaging in sexually assaultive behavior often had delinquent peers with attitudes accepting criminal behavior in general, and sexual offending in particular. The Ageton sample appears to have predominantly included individuals who offended sexually against peers.

In their follow-up recidivism study among AISB, Proulx and Carpentier (2011) did not find that association with delinquent peers was related to sexual recidivism, although they did find an association with nonsexual recidivism. As noted earlier, however, having an antisocial orientation can be a risk factor for repeated sexual offending for some adolescents, and it is a strong risk factor for nonsexual reoffending; thus, when negative or delinquent peer relationships are present, disrupting these relationships in favor of pro-social ties is an important criminogenic need that, if effectively addressed, can help reduce recidivism.

Use of leisure time. In their meta-analysis, Cottle et al. (2001) found a strong effect size for poor use of leisure time and general delinquency (i.e., statistical analyses indicated they were strongly related). Similarly, Hawkins et al. (2000) found isolation from conventional pro-social pursuits related to the risk of violent behavior. It does not appear that the relationship between the use of leisure time and sexual reoffending has been specifically explored; however, data suggest that sexual assaults by adolescents occur most frequently in the afternoon, a time of day when they are expected to be in school or afterward, times when caregivers and other adults may be less available owing to work or additional responsibilities (National Incident-Based Reporting System, 2004, as cited by Finkelhor et al., 2009).

Further, Spice et al. (2013) found the opportunity to offend was the only significant risk factor associated with sexual reoffending in their study. Together, these findings reflect the importance of interventions that not only facilitate pro-social ties but provide sufficient structure, support, and supervision to reduce opportunities for reoffending, while fostering healthy and positive adolescent development. (See the "Social Bonds & Orientation" subsection of appendix A: Criminogenic Treatment Targets: Summary Table.)

General Self-Regulation

Problems with self-regulation include difficulties with concentration, impulse and emotional control, restlessness and hyperactivity, substance abuse, and risk taking. Problems with self-regulation are associated with a wide range of challenges including learning difficulties, problematic parent–child relationships, peer rejection, aggression (Ford, Chapman, Conner, & Cruise, 2012; Kendall & Braswell, 1993), delinquency (e.g., Lipsey & Derzon, 1998) and violence (e.g., Hawkins et al., 2000). These challenges may interfere with one's ability to be successful in school, at work, and interpersonally.

As Carpentier and Proulx (2011) observed, adolescents with poor behavioral self-control tend to avoid situations of social control where they experience supervision and discipline. Consequently, self-regulation problems may interfere with an adolescent's ability to participate effectively and successfully in treatment, in placements, or with conditions of probation or parole. Thus, general self-regulation problems may not only be a criminogenic need, but a responsivity factor as well for interventions (see chapter 3: Increasing Positive Treatment Outcomes—Responsivity).

Self-regulation deficits. The risk relevance of self-regulation problems for sexual reoffending was demonstrated in a study comparing adults who began sexually offending as juveniles and who continued into adulthood, with those who began their offending as adults. Knight and Prentky (1993) found that those who began as juveniles and persisted showed greater impulsivity than those who began offending sexually later in life. Other research studies have indicated that greater problems with self-regulation among AISB are associated with increased sexual recidivism. For example, in a sample of juveniles, those with a "self-regulation disorder" (e.g., attention deficit / hyperactivity disorder, conduct disorder, or oppositional defiant disorder) had higher rates of sexual recidivism than those without such a disorder (Epperson et al., 2006). Similarly, self-control problems, restlessness, concentration problems, and risk taking have been associated with violent offending (Hawkins et al., 1998; Herrenkohl et al., 2007).

In Hanson and Morton-Bourgon's (2005) meta-analysis of mostly adults with sex offenses, general self-regulation problems were strongly associated with sexual recidivism. General self-regulation problems included measures of impulsivity, lifestyle instability, and Factor 2 of the *Psychopathy Checklist Revised* (Hare et al., 1990). General self-regulation problems also were very strongly associated with any type of reoffending.

Impulsivity. In a recent study of risk and protective factors, Spice et al. (2013) did not find impulsivity or any other risk or protective factors identified in the adolescent sexual or violent risk assessment literature to be associated with sexual reoffending, except "opportunity to offend." Yet, it stands to reason that, when provided with an opportunity to offend, one can be thoughtful and consider the consequences of such behavior and choose not to act, or to act, perhaps impulsively, and take advantage of the perceived opportunity. The impulsivity variable used in this study was a measure of "very poor" self-regulation of affect and behavior during the past six months at discharge from a residential treatment center. The absence of a positive finding might reflect that the controlled setting of a residential treatment program helped the youths regulate themselves more successfully than when back in the community.

Most studies of AISB use combined measures of impulsivity and antisocial behaviors (e.g., Parks & Bard, 2006; Waite, 2005). In such instances it is not possible to tease out general self-regulation problems from an antisocial orientation. Epperson et al. (2006), however, found impulsivity was associated with sexual recidivism. Carpentier and Proulx (2011) found attention deficit hyperactivity disorder, which they described as an indicator of impulsivity or low self-control, was positively associated with violent, nonsexual reoffending but not sexual reoffending.

Academic behavior problems. Academic and school experiences of AISB vary. Some AISB perform well in school, while many experience academic difficulties such as disruptive behavior, truancy, academic problems, learning disabilities, and placement in special classes (Fehrenbach, Smith, Monastersky, & Deisher, 1986; Kahn & Chambers, 1991; Miner, Siekert, & Ackland, 1997). Academic and school difficulties may not necessarily be due to the youth's intellectual and cognitive abilities, but may also be related to factors such as attention difficulties, impulsivity, and conduct problems.

Several studies have found academic difficulties related to sexual recidivism. For example, Epperson et al. (2006) found placement in special education and disciplinary problems in school to be associated with higher rates of sexual recidivism. Wiebush (1996) found a significant relationship between special education status and sexual recidivism, but did not find a significant relationship for school behavior problems. Conversely, Schram et al. (1991) found those who committed new sexual or nonsexual offenses were more likely to have school behavior problems or truancy.

Problems with school attendance, truancy, school affiliation, and active involvement, as well as achievement, also have been associated with violent reoffending (Hawkins et al., 1998). In a meta-analysis of risk factors associated with any type of reoffending among adolescents with general delinquency, Cottle et al. (2001) found placement in special education classes was associated with general recidivism, but other school-related variables, such as school attendance, were not related to recidivism.

Substance abuse. Substance abuse may reflect poor self-regulation and contribute to a variety of personal, family, and social problems. As noted previously, similar to the adult sex-offending literature (Hanson & Morton-Bourgon, 2005), additional research (e.g., Knight & Sims-Knight, 2004; van der Put et al., 2013) indicates that AISB who assaulted peer-aged or adult victims frequently evidence greater criminal histories, conduct problems, antisocial attitudes and beliefs, delinquent peer associations, and substance abuse than those who targeted children.

Meta-analytic studies of general delinquency recidivism have identified substance abuse as a strong risk factor for general reoffending (e.g., Heilbrun et al., 2005). Meta-analytic studies of sexual recidivism (e.g., Hanson & Bourgon, 2005; McCann & Lussier, 2008) have not specifically explored the utility of substance abuse as a risk factor for repeated sexual offending. Instead, substance abuse problems have been included in composite measures of an antisocial orientation.

Studies have found substance abuse to be a problem for some AISB (Kahn & Chambers, 1991; Miner et al., 1997). For some adolescents it may be a relevant factor in the initial sexual offense and possibly, in some instances, it may be related to sexual reoffending, while for others substance abuse may not be linked to sexual offending at all. In spite of the limited research on this topic, it is notable that Carpentier, Leclerc, and Proulx (2011) found that AISB with fewer substance abuse problems were less likely to sexually recidivate.

Substance abuse problems are relevant treatment targets as dynamic risk factors for treatment responsiveness as well as recidivism. Substance abuse can have a disinhibiting effect on both sexual and aggressive behavior (see Seto & Barbaree, 1995) and can exacerbate problems such as poor impulse control, problem-solving challenges, and social-skills deficits. As a result of these effects, substance abuse may increase the risk of sexual reoffending for some AISB (Lightfoot & Barbaree, 1993). Those with very serious substance abuse problems may require intensive drug and alcohol treatment, sometimes prior to treatment efforts related to sex offending (Lightfoot & Barbaree).

Emotional self-regulation. The ability to effectively express emotions requires identifying one's own feelings correctly as well as those of others, expressing one's feelings accurately, and managing and modulating emotions so they may be interpreted correctly. Difficulty understanding and expressing emotions has been associated with risky behavior (Hessler & Katz, 2010), difficulty seeking help among adolescents (Ciarrochi, Deane, Wilson, & Rickwood, 2002), and psychopathy in adults (Rogstad & Rogers, 2008).

Hanson and Harris (2000) found that increased negative mood and anger were antecedents to sexual offending among adults. Also, in a small study of adults, Proulx, McKibben, and Lusignan (1996) found that anger (especially for the rapists) or negative affect (such as loneliness and humiliation) preceded masturbation to deviant fantasies. In addition, some retrospective studies of AISB have found recent escalations in negative emotions such as anger, frustration, loneliness, sadness, boredom, worthlessness, and feeling rejected are immediate precursors to their sex offending (Worling & Långström, 2003).

Difficulty identifying, expressing, and coping with negative emotions may contribute to adolescent violent behavior (Marohn, 1992). In addition, Howel, Reddon, and Enns (1997) found that emotions such as depression, hopelessness, and feeling rejected or isolated from parents or peers were immediate precursors to general recidivism among adolescents.

It is important to remember, however, that acquiring emotional and self-regulation are developmental processes associated with brain development, which continues into young adulthood (Bonnie & Scott, 2013). As will be discussed in chapter 3, developmentally appropriate interventions to facilitate effective self-regulation can be important treatment targets to address both criminogenic needs and facilitate responsivity. (See the "General Self-Regulation" subsection of appendix A: Criminogenic Treatment Targets: Summary Table.)

Social Competence

Social competence refers to the social, emotional, cognitive, and behavioral skills required to successfully develop and maintain productive relationships with others. Adolescents who lack social competence may have difficulties deciding on appropriate behavior for different situations, interpreting social cues successfully under various circumstances, and anticipating the consequences for one's own behavior, or the behavior of others (Westling, Andrew, & Peterson, 2012). Deficits in these areas have been linked with oppositional defiant disorders and misbehavior in early childhood, conduct disorders and delinquency in adolescence, and illegal behavior in adulthood (Reid, 1993).

Social and intimate relationships. In their meta-analysis, Seto and Lalumière (2010) explored social problems among a large sample of AISB and those who committed other types of offenses. They focused on social problems that can interfere with the development or maintenance of relationships. AISB tended to have more heterosocial-skills deficits (most AISB identify as heterosexual), general social-skills deficits, and general or other social problems than adolescents with nonsexual offenses, but differed significantly only in social isolation.

Recently, Miner et al. (2010) found that, compared with adolescents who committed sexual offenses against women or peer-aged girls, or those who committed nonsexual offenses, adolescents who had sexually offended against younger children had greater attachment anxiety and were more socially isolated from their female peers. They concluded that these adolescents may turn to young children to satisfy not only their sexual needs but intimacy needs as well, and may fear that age-mates will reject them, as has been proposed regarding adults who sexually abuse children (Ward, Hudson, Marshall, & Siegert, 1995). The tendency to prefer the company of children, and to feel more comfortable emotionally and interpersonally with children, has been described in the adult sex-offending literature as "emotional congruence with children" or "emotional identification with children" and will be discussed further below (see McPhail, Hermann, & Nunes, 2013; Seto, 2008).

Conflicts in interpersonal relationships may interfere with the ability to maintain friendships, develop new relationships, and establish satisfying mutual, age-appropriate intimacy. For some adolescents, social-skills deficits and low self-esteem may limit self-confidence and the ability to develop age-appropriate peer relationships, as well as age-appropriate intimate relationships and sexual activities with consenting partners.

Yet surprisingly little research has explored adolescent dating and intimate relationships, perhaps because adolescence spans such a wide age range (e.g., ages 12 to 17), and interest in intimate relationships is just beginning for some adolescents. It is therefore important to consider these potential risk factors with a developmental perspective. Even with adults, however, aside from marital status, research studies exploring the intimate relationships of adults with sex offenses also have been limited (Hanson & Bourgon, 2005).

In their meta-analysis of follow-up studies, Hanson & Morton-Bourgon (2005) developed a composite variable that included poor social skills, negative social influences, conflicts in intimate relationships, emotional identification with children, and loneliness. They found a small but significant association between the composite variable and recidivism rates, with substantial variability among its components. Large associations were found for conflicts in intimate relationships and emotional identification with children.

Social isolation. Social isolation can be due to a variety of factors, including geography, transportation access, and family resources. As mentioned above, Seto and Lalumière (2010) found in their meta-analysis comparing adolescents with sex offenses and those with other types of offending that AISB experienced greater social isolation than adolescents who committed nonsexual crimes. Findings from studies regarding the social relationships of AISB and recidivism rates, however, have been mixed.

Långström and Grann (2000) found that adolescents[1] who had limited social contacts were three times more likely to reoffend sexually. Worling and Curwen (2000), however, found no relationship between self-described rates of social involvement and sexual recidivism. They wondered if self-reported peer relationships may not be a reliable measure of existing relationships because teenagers may have difficulty acknowledging social difficulties. A recent pro-

---

1 Defined in this sample as persons aged 15 to 20.

spective study investigating the validity of the Estimated Risk of Adolescent Sexual Recidivism Risk (ERASOR) (Worling et al., 2012) found an item included in the ERASOR that measures a lack of intimate peer relationships and social isolation was associated with sexual reoffending. In contrast, however, Spice et al. (2013) did not find this same item associated with sexual recidivism.

Additionally, Långström and Grann (2000) found "poor social skills" (defined by the authors as limited extra-familial social experiences exampled by no more than one of the following: peer group membership, having had a girlfriend or boyfriend, adult contact other than parents, and leisure time outside the home) were positively associated with sexual reoffending. These variables appear to reflect social isolation rather than poor social skills per se and may, consistent with Worling et al. (2012), suggest social difficulties resulting in social isolation may be more of a risk factor, than social-skills deficits.

In a retrospective study, Kenny et al. (2001) found adolescents with social-skills problems had sexually abused more victims than those who did not. Social-skills problems were defined by a composite variable that included social isolation and withdrawal, peer intimidation and rejection, as well as interviewer assessments of social skills (e.g., eye contact, quality of engagement, and verbalizations). The authors combined these items to create a yes/no "poor social skills" variable, which as such does not provide evidence that social-skills deficits are criminogenic risk factors for sexual reoffending. It may be that, as Hawkins et al. (2000) observed, some adolescents who feel rejected and marginalized from pro-social peers find delinquent friends to associate with, whereas others, as Carpentier and Proulx (2011) suggested, turn to younger children who are more accepting of them and less judgmental.

Emotional congruence with children. Emotional identification or congruence with children typically involves an adult who identifies more with children than peers and prefers associating with children to meet interpersonal, affective, and intimacy needs (McPhail et al., 2013). Emotional congruence with children has long been theorized to be a risk factor for child sexual abuse in adult offending models (Finkelhor, 1984). Meta-analytic results (e.g., Hanson & Morton-Bourgon, 2005) have found a strong association between emotional congruence with children and sexual recidivism. Although the relevance of this risk factor may appear less clear for AISB who have more in common with children than adults and whose developmental age may not reflect their chronological age (as with an emotionally immature or developmentally delayed adolescent), a preference for associating with significantly younger children may still be a risk factor for sexual reoffending among AISB.

Recently, McPhail et al. (2013) conducted a meta-analysis that specifically explored the relationship between emotional congruence with children and sexual reoffending. They found that men with extrafamilial victims, and particularly boy victims, had higher rates of emotional congruence with children. They also found higher rates of emotional congruence with children were moderately associated with sexual recidivism, but this association was especially strong for those with extrafamilial boy victims. Encouragingly, McPhail et al. found that emotional congruence could be effectively targeted with treatment. Comparisons of pre- and posttreatment measures showed significant changes in this dynamic risk factor.

The McPhail et al. (2013) meta-analysis included only one study of adolescents. Recently, Carpentier and Proulx (2012) found that associating with significantly younger children was a specific risk factor for sexual recidivism among AISB. Because adolescents are still developing cognitively, emotionally, and socially, interventions with these youths may be even more effective than has been found by McPhail et al. with adults. (See the "Social Competence" subsection of appendix A: Criminogenic Treatment Targets: Summary Table.)

Socio-Ecological Factors

Our approach to understanding dynamic risk and protective factors in AISB, and intervening effectively, is based on a multisystemic framework. Adolescents are interconnected with their families, peers, and communities; thus, in addition to individual factors, family, community risk, and protective factors also must be considered. For example, some AISB may already be involved with social service or juvenile justice agencies, and the extent to which the adolescent or his or her family perceives these professionals or other service providers as helpful or stressful varies and may be an important consideration. Others may have exhibited sexual behavior problems in school, or their offending may be known in school, and they may be ostracized as a result. In such instances, multisystemic interventions at the individual, family, and other socio-ecological levels and domains may be required to achieve positive outcomes.

Families and caregivers. Families and caregivers of AISB, like the youths themselves, are heterogeneous. Their family histories and current circumstances differ, as do the abilities of caregivers to provide necessary support and supervision. Studies indicate that family separations and instability, substance abuse, parental psychopathology, criminality, and violence are prevalent in some samples (cf. Righthand & Welch, 2004). Although parent–child relationships vary, some parents have been described as disengaged, rejecting, and physically and/or emotionally inaccessible to their children (Miner & Crimmins, 1995; Smith & Israel, 1987; Worling et al., 2012). Adequate parental support and appropriate supervision may be lacking (Borduin, Henggeler, Blaske, & Stein, 1990; Borduin, Schaeffer, & Heiblum, 2009; Henggeler et al., 2009). In addition, parent–child communications may be hostile and problematic overall (Blaske, Borduin, Henggeler, & Mann, 1989; Henggeler et al., 2009; Worling et al., 2012).

AISB do not differ significantly on many family characteristics from adolescents who have committed other types of offenses. Seto and Lalumière's (2010) meta-analytic findings indicated these two groups did not differ on family relationship problems, family member substance abuse or criminality, or parent–child separation. Some studies have found that levels of family cohesion and adaptability for both AISB as well as adolescents whose delinquency is limited to nonsexual offending are significantly lower than adolescents with no known offending (Bischof, Stith, & Whitney, 1995; Bischof, Stith, & Wilson, 1992; Blaske et al., 1989; Ronis & Borduin, 2007; van Wijk et al., 2005). The importance of family factors such as caregivers' abilities to adequately support and supervise their children who are involved in the juvenile justice system is indicated by meta-analytic findings concerning adolescents with a variety of offenses. Cottle et al. (2001) found that poor family relationships and difficulties, as well as the number of out-of-home placements, were associated with repeat offending of any kind. Regarding AISB, Spice et al. (2013) explored a variety of risk and protective factors associated with sexual and nonsexual recidivism. They found only opportunities to reoffend (e.g., insufficient monitoring of the adolescents' whereabouts, unsupervised access to potential victims, and caregivers unaware of or unconcerned with possible risk factors) were significantly associated with sexual recidivism. Although Spice did not find parental rejection or conflict to be associated with sexual reoffending, Worling et al. (2012) and Worling and Curwen (2000) did find this variable to be a risk factor. Additionally, Carpentier and Proulx (2011) found long-term paternal abandonment was associated with sexual reoffending. Thus, it may be that conflicting parent–child relationships, rejection, and abandonment contribute to opportunities to reoffend through insufficient parental availability, monitoring, and support.

Not all families of adolescents with sexual offending histories experience significant difficulties or have members who exhibit dysfunctional behaviors (Chaffin & Bonner, 1998). Yet, when family factors and parent–adolescent relationships are problematic, or when life stresses may exceed parent and caregiver's abilities to adequately supervise and support their children, research findings suggest that effective interventions may reduce sexual and nonsexual recidivism.

Community ties. A variety of community-level factors may increase or mitigate the risk of sexual and nonsexual offending. For example, poverty and community disorganization may limit the ability of adults to provide sufficient monitoring and supervision, or to engage youths in pro-social pursuits. Family or neighbors' involvement in crime or violence may model antisocial values and behaviors that support offending. In addition, media and cultural attitudes that objectify and sexualize children, teens, as well as adults may contribute to attitudes and beliefs that support sexual abuse. On a more positive note, however, the field of general delinquency research has shown that having a positive adult role model is associated with less recidivism (Werner, 1993). Pro-social community members can engage youth in positive activities and provide mentoring opportunities that may, for example, facilitate a pro-social orientation and social competence, which are factors associated with sexual and nonsexual recidivism.

Factors such as frequent school changes, truancy, limited bonding to school, and dropping out are associated with youth violence (Hawkins et al., 2000). Schram et al. (1991) found truancy to be associated with sexual recidivism among adolescents who have sexually offended. Knight et al. (2009) found that juveniles who persisted in sexually offending into adulthood had greater junior high school behavior problems than those who began sexually offending as adults. Further, the potential relevance of school engagement as a protective factor associated with reoffending is suggested by Carpentier et al. (2011), who found adolescents with lower rates of school behavior problems and school failure were most likely to have no new offenses of any kind.

Although some AISB are not old enough to have part-time or stable employment opportunities, some are. Sampson & Laub (2003) found adolescents with histories of delinquency, who obtain stable employment, have lower recidivism rates. Work opportunities may provide pro-social affiliation, increased social competence, and improved use of leisure time, all or some of which may be relevant criminogenic treatment targets for individual adolescents.

Summary of socio-ecological factors. In a recent large study of risk factors associated with reoffending, van der Put et al. (2012) found that the relative importance of dynamic risk factors varied with adolescent development. Family factors were most influential during childhood and early adolescence, whereas peer relationships became more influential as youths entered their teenage years. Other factors, such as pro-criminal attitudes and engagement and performance in school, became more significant in later adolescence as well. Van der Put et al. also found strong interrelationships between individual risk factors and family, school, and social relationships, providing additional support for the importance of multisystemic interventions.

In sum, research with AISB reflects that factors associated with problematic sexual behavior as well as with delinquency are not limited to individual characteristics of the adolescents, but include other domains such as family, school, peers, and community. Thus, holistic, socio-ecological interventions are likely to be most successful in assisting adolescents who have offended sexually develop and fulfill pro-social lifestyles (Henggeler et al., 2009). (See the "Socio-Ecological Factors" subsection of appendix A: Criminogenic Treatment Targets: Summary Table.)

3 Increasing Positive Treatment Outcomes—Responsivity

Introduction

As noted in chapter 1, the risk-need-responsivity (RNR) model describes three major principles of correctional rehabilitation and human-services delivery that, if met, are associated with greater reductions in criminal recidivism among adults (Andrews & Bonta, 2010) and juveniles (e.g., Pealer & Latessa, 2004), as well as adults and juveniles who have committed sexual offenses (Hanson et al., 2009). Whereas the *risk principle* provides that resources will be most effectively utilized when they are focused on those *who* present with the most risks and needs, the *need principle* emphasizes that interventions that target dynamic risk and protective factors associated with recidivism will be most successful; that is, the need principle describes the *what* of treatment. Chapter 2 presented a review of the dynamic factors that are important targets of treatment.

The *responsivity principle* recognizes that, to be most effective, interventions must attend to individual or family characteristics, such as learning styles. One size does not fit all. Interventions that are tailored to relevant individual and familial characteristics, such as motivation to change, learning strengths and challenges, and co-occurring disorders, may increase engagement and retention in treatment and facilitate positive outcomes; that is, responsivity concerns *how* to provide interventions. In this section, we will focus on the responsivity principle and review some of the responsivity needs of adolescents who have offended sexually, and their families. Treatment responsivity includes both static and dynamic factors that may facilitate therapeutic engagement and our clients' abilities to make use of our interventions.

Developmental Factors

Understanding the developmental differences between adolescents and adults is of paramount importance for understanding adolescent behavior and supporting healthy development. Although a thorough review of adolescent developmental research is beyond the scope of this book, research (see, for example, Bonnie & Scott, 2013; Steinberg, 2007; Steinberg & Scott, 2003) has shown that, compared with adults, adolescents generally are more impulsive, have poorer judgment, and are less able to consider the future consequences of their behavior. Adolescents also tend to be more self-focused and self-absorbed, and may be less able to accurately identify the emotions of others, which can contribute to misinterpretations of social cues and may contribute to inappropriate responses or behavior.

Developmental differences between young adolescents and older adolescents also are apparent in their cognitive, emotional, social, and behavioral skills and abilities (e.g., Modecki, 2008; Monahan, Steinberg, & Cauffman, 2009). Individual youth not only vary in how quickly or slowly they mature, but may develop more quickly in some domains than others. Developmentally appropriate interventions that fit the adolescent's developmental age and levels of maturity are required.

Adolescence is an important time period for self-concept and identity formation. Thus, it is important not only to build on the youth's strengths and successes, but also to be sensitive to how terminology and labels, such as the term *juvenile sex offender*, can be harmful. Although we must label abusive behavior for what it is, it is important to use person-first language that helps clients see and believe they are more than their offenses (Righthand & Welch, 2001).

Motivation and Change

Stopping problematic behavior requires motivation or desire to change. As Prochaska, DiClemente, and Norcross (1992) pointed out regarding stages of change in addressing health-related behaviors, some people may not believe they have a problem or may not perceive a need to change. Others may contemplate the possibility that there is a problem, but not be ready to engage in behavioral change. Still others may be actively engaged in altering problematic behaviors or maintaining the changes they already have made. External controls may help curtail sexual and other types of offending, but altering thoughts, emotions, and behaviors associated with offending, and developing attitudes and values incompatible with offending behaviors, are most likely to facilitate lasting change.

Although Hanson and Morton-Bourgon's (2005) meta-analytic findings indicated that low motivation for treatment at time of intake was not related to sexual recidivism, developing therapeutic alliances, engaging clients in treatment, and building motivation for change are important first steps for effective interventions (e.g., Marshall, 2005). As indicated by the most recent Safer Society Foundation survey of treatment providers (McGrath et al., 2010), less than half of adolescent and adult community-based programs reported utilizing strategies such as motivational interviewing to facilitate interventions. Residential treatment programs for adolescents were more likely to report using such strategies; however, only 57 percent of these interventions were designed to facilitate, enhance, or maintain motivation.

When working with adolescents, family engagement and interventions are of great importance (e.g., Henggeler et al., 2009). Family members often are reluctant or resistant to treatment involvement, perhaps believing that it is the child alone who has problems. Some families may not even be supportive of their child's treatment involvement (e.g., Kimball & Guarino-Ghezzi, 1996). Thus, motivating family members to also participate in treatment may be essential for increasing treatment engagement and positive treatment outcomes.

Responsibility and Change

Responsibility, as defined here, refers to the adolescent increasingly developing an internal locus of control and taking charge of making risk-relevant changes in his or her thinking, emotions, and behaviors. In a recent study comparing two groups of adults who had offended against children, Farmer, Beech, and Ward (2012) found that individuals who appeared to have stopped offending described an enhanced sense of personal agency, a more internalized locus of control, as well as optimism about the future. These men considered treatment as a turning point in their lives. In contrast, individuals whom the researchers thought might still be offending were more pessimistic in their outlook and tended to externalize blame and responsibility for their problems. As with motivation and readiness for change, assuming personal responsibility for one's own behavior is a developmental task that increases with adolescent maturation processes and may be facilitated by positive therapeutic alliances and treatment strategies.

Many practitioners who work with adolescents, as well as those who work with adults, consider accepting responsibility for one's sexual-offending behavior to be one of the most important components—often the first step—in sex-offense-specific treatment (McGrath et al., 2010). Some programs require admissions and, particularly in the United States, detailed disclosures that are consistent with official reports for treatment completion. Research supporting this requirement, however, is lacking. Although admitting to an offense may enable a functional analysis of the antecedent thoughts, feelings, and behaviors associated with an offense, and may provide useful safety planning information, meta-analytic findings have not demonstrated an association between whether someone denied sexual offending and sexual recidivism (Hanson & Morton-Bourgon, 2005). Targeting empirically based risk and protective factors associated with offending may be more effective (Marshall, Thornton, Marshall, Fernandez, & Mann, 2001).

Denying and minimizing one's offense may be risk-relevant for a subset of individuals who offend sexually. For example, Nunes and colleagues (Nunes et al., 2007) found increased sexual recidivism rates among fathers who sexually abused their own children and were persistent in categorical denial. Also, in a study of adults considered to be at high risk of sexual reoffending, Langton et al. (2008) found minimizing sexual offending behaviors was a significant predictor of sexual recidivism for this high-risk group. In an adolescent sample, Epperson et al. (2006) found that denying or minimizing offense responsibility, *at the time of discharge* from treatment, was positively associated with sexual recidivism.

Complicating matters further, several studies have indicated that AISB who denied their offenses were *less* likely to sexually reoffend (Kahn & Chambers, 1991; Långström & Grann, 2000; Smith & Monastersky, 1986; Worling, 2002). For example, Kahn and Chambers (1991) found that of the eight adolescents who completely denied their sexual offenses, none reoffended sexually. Further, Smith and Monastersky (1986) found that a willingness to discuss the referral sexual offense non-defensively was associated with an *increased* likelihood of sexual reoffending. Although these studies are small in size, their findings—combined with the absence of strong research indicating that adolescents who deny their sex offense present a greater risk of sexual reoffending—raise serious questions about interventions that mandate adolescents admit their sexual offending.

To help understand the lack of association between denial and sexual recidivism in most studies, Worling and Långström (2003) postulated that some adolescents who deny their sexual offenses might have a greater antisocial orientation than others. They explain further that these adolescents may be less likely to commit additional sexual offenses because their sex offending was opportunistic rather than indicative of persistent atypical interests in illegal sexual conduct. Another possible explanation for the lack of a positive association between denying a sex offense and sexual recidivism may be that some adolescents deny their sexual offenses because they internally accept responsibility for what they did, but are ashamed of their abusive behavior. This shame and self-blame may motivate them to stop their sexually abusive behaviors (consider Tangney, Stuewig, & Martinez, 2014), perhaps even without additional interventions. In contrast, some adolescents who may be more likely to continue sexual offending may enjoy talking about their sexual offenses, possibly becoming sexually aroused while doing so.

Whether the adolescent admits sexually offending during treatment or not may not be important. What may be most important is whether the adolescent demonstrates increased personal responsibility by identifying and addressing empirically based risk and protective factors in his or her life. Increasing positive peer relationships and activities, managing risk factors and facilitating protective factors related to offending, and valuing and living pro-social lifestyles are associated with desistence from crime.

While admitting one's offense does not appear to be necessary for risk reduction or treatment responsivity in most cases, in situations involving intrafamilial sexual abuse, acknowledging and making amends for abusive behavior is considered an important step before family reconciliation, reunification, and reintegration can occur (Bonner, 2009; Thomas, 1997; Thomas & Viar, 2005). When family members are reunited on outings or home visits, and when reunification in the home is a consideration, these activities are approached cautiously, with a priority on the safety and security of each child in the home, and with special concern for the child who was sexually abused by the adolescent. The emotional and physical safety of all the children are of great importance; having the adolescent clarify what abusive behaviors occurred, his or her personal responsibility, what he or she is doing to prevent a reoccurrence, and his or her current appreciation of how the abuse has affected and hurt family members can be important for creating useful safety plans, repairing and developing respect and trust among family members, and facilitating family relationships.

Learning Styles and Cognitive Abilities

Adolescence is a time of rapid cognitive development. Maturation and improvements in abstract reasoning, such as delaying gratification for future benefits, thinking about the longer-term consequences of one's behavior, and taking another's perspective are expected.

Adolescents who offend sexually vary in cognitive abilities, learning styles, and challenges. These differences are of great importance because, although they are not directly related to reoffending, such factors can interfere with the adolescent's ability to engage in and use treatment effectively. Even if someone is motivated for treatment and invested in positive behavior change, interventions must be provided in a manner that is developmentally appropriate and matched to his or her learning styles.

Ferrara and McDonald (1996) indicated, however, that research pertaining to juveniles who have committed any type of delinquent offenses has noted two primary areas of impairment: (*a*) difficulties with executive functions, such as planning, abstraction, inhibition of inappropriate impulses, and cognitive flexibility, and (*b*) difficulties with receptive and expressive language. Based on their literature review, Ferrara and McDonald concluded that between one-quarter and one-third of AISB might have some form of neurological impairment.

Many AISB have experienced learning difficulties in school, special education placements, academic failure, and school dropout (e.g., Carpentier et al., 2012; Cottle et al., 2001; Hawkins et al., 2000). As a consequence of such negative experiences, learning opportunities such as treatment may be devalued, avoided when possible, and met with expectations for failure.

Multimodal, active learning opportunities (cf. Ferrara & McDonald, 1996; Page & Murphy, 2007) that utilize cognitive-behavioral and social-learning approaches may be best for facilitating skill development and targeting problematic attitudes and beliefs (Andrews & Bonta, 2010). Interventions that identify and build on a client's learning-style strengths and abilities, help make learning interesting and enjoyable (when possible), and provide opportunities for success are likely to be most effective.

Mental Health and Behavioral Health Challenges and Co-Occurring Disorders

AISB vary as to whether they have symptoms or diagnoses of mental disorders. Symptoms may be situational and related to being caught following their abusive behavior. Other times, their difficulties are more chronic. Mental health challenges can compromise personal strengths, competence, and learning abilities. They also can interfere with treatment engagement and progress and, therefore, must be adequately addressed prior to or concurrent with interventions that address criminogenic needs.

Few studies of AISB have found major psychopathology in the youths or their families (Righthand & Welch, 2001). However, Seto and Lalumière's (2010) meta-analysis indicated that AISB evidenced significantly more problematic psychological symptoms related to anxiety, social anxiety, and self-esteem than those with other forms of illegal behavior. Other studies have found that, in comparison with the general adolescent population, AISB exhibit higher rates of depressive symptoms, with a significant number of adolescents who have histories of childhood physical abuse or sexual abuse appearing to be severely depressed (Becker & Hunter, 1997). If sexual victimization histories are related to depression among these teens, Seto and Lalumière's (2010) finding that adolescents with sex-offending histories have more than five times greater odds of having been sexually abused than those who had committed nonsexual offenses may help explain the trend to higher rates of depression among AISB.

Some adolescents may have symptoms of post-traumatic stress disorder or complex trauma that contributes to cognitive, emotional, or behavioral dysregulation. For example, intrusive thoughts or some treatment topics (e.g., group discussions about childhood abuse) may trigger memories of the adolescent's personal experiences as a victim and contribute to emotional or behavioral dysregulation (Hunter, Figueredo, & Malamuth, 2010). This dysregulation may be an obstacle to treatment, for example, when maltreatment experiences impair trust and the ability to establish therapeutic alliances, positive mentoring relationships with adults, or positive peer relationships.

When considering someone's history of maltreatment or trauma, it is important to remember that most people who have had such experiences do not harm others. Further, adverse life experiences have not been found to be associated with reoffending (Hanson & Morton-Bougon, 2005). Yet, if an adolescent's experiences as a victim of maltreatment are interfering with his or her ability to engage effectively in needed interventions, trauma-focused treatment may help facilitate positive treatment outcomes. Similarly, if depression, anxiety, or other co-occurring psychological problems or disorders interfere with treatment engagement or progression, appropriate interventions are indicated.

Attention deficit disorder (ADD) with or without hyperactivity (ADHD) and learning disorders also may interfere with an adolescent's ability to engage in and benefit from treatment. As described in the section on cognitive functioning above, interventions must be tailored to the individual's learning style and strengths. Accommodations for learning challenges may be needed. For example, an adolescent with ADHD may need to be allowed to get out of his seat and move around or have something to fidget with in his hands while participating in treatment. Active, multimodal treatment interventions may increase attention and treatment engagement, not only for adolescents with ADD/ADHD, but for adolescents in general.

Developmental disabilities such as autism spectrum disorders are sometimes identified because of sex-offending behaviors. Problems understanding social rules, interpreting social cues correctly, and accurately communicating with potential sex partners can contribute to sexual behaviors that are socially inappropriate and/or illegal (see Timms & Goreczny, 2002). The likelihood of problematic behavior may be greatest when adolescents with developmental disabilities are not provided with adequate education about sexual behavior norms, instruction that can help them express romantic interests and urges appropriately, as well as when they are socially isolated from age-appropriate partners. Although some adolescents with developmental disabilities may have atypical sexual interests, as with most adolescents, the majority of youth with developmental disabilities are likely to have normative sexual interests.

Holistic assessments that involve caregivers and identify the adolescent's strengths and challenges, risk and protective factors, and treatment responsivity needs can help determine the best interventions for a particular individual and identify specific treatment strategies. Lindsay (2005) suggests that when working with people who have developmental disabilities, treatment interventions facilitate developing appropriate sexual outlets, improving self-regulation, and increasing social engagement in order to provide more opportunities for positive and pro-social interactions. These treatment targets are consistent with the criminogenic needs discussed throughout this book. In addition, consistent with the responsivity principle and as Ferrara and McDonald (1996) noted, treatment interventions with people who have learning challenges must be individually tailored to be effective and must be delivered in a manner that encourages learning and promotes attention, concentration, recall, and generalizing beyond the therapeutic context.

For example, when cognitive challenges are present, interventions must be provided in a manner that facilitates and maximizes learning. Lindsay (2005) suggests a focus of treatment on appropriate sexual outlets, improving self-regulation, and increasing social engagement in order to provide more opportunities for positive and pro-social interactions. Social engagement includes supporting and facilitating vocational, social, and leisure activities.

Summary of mental health challenges. Although serious mental health challenges typically are not directly related to sexual or nonsexual recidivism, AISB may obtain optimal benefit from treatment only when their cognitive and mental health challenges are identified and adequately addressed. For example, an adolescent who is depressed and feels hopeless may have difficulty engaging in treatment. When mental disorders are present and interfere with offense-specific interventions, they must be addressed to facilitate treatment responsivity and positive outcomes. If such challenges are unrelated to offending and are outside the service provider's area of expertise, consultation or appropriate referrals are indicated.

Additional Considerations

Additional considerations may include factors such as gender and culture as well as other unique factors that can affect treatment engagement and success.

Gender. The vast majority of AISB are male (e.g., Finkelhor et al., 2009) and thus research concerning female AISB is very limited. Professionals who work with female AISB are encouraged to read reviews by Gannon and Cortoni (2010) and Ryan, Hunter, and Murrie (2012). It is also recommended that professionals be aware of current debates about the necessity and utility of gender-specific interventions (e.g., Chamberlain, Leve, & DeGarmo, 2007; Hubbard & Matthews, 2008; Ogden & Hagen, 2009; Zahn, Day, Mihalic, & Tichavsky, 2009).

Culture. Individual, family, and community values and beliefs influence adolescents. When working with AISB and their families, it is necessary for professionals to recognize that cultural attitudes and practices—which can be influenced by ethnicity, religion, social class, and language—affect treatment engagement and outcome. Effective interventions require practitioners to become knowledgeable of the families' cultural attitudes and practices and to make interventions accessible to families accordingly. When practitioners and families have conflicting viewpoints, it is important to address these differences sensitively and in a collaborative manner.

4 Assessment—Risk and Needs Assessment Measures

Identifying risks, criminogenic needs, and responsivity factors are important components of initial clinical assessment and reassessment. Such assessment is necessary for case management, treatment planning, and legal decision making. An exhaustive review of assessment practices for AISB, however, is beyond the scope of this book. (Interested readers may find the following books and other resources on assessing adolescents useful, for example: Barbaree & Marshall, 2006; Rich, 2009; Rich, 2011; Ryan et al., 2012; Worling & Langton, 2012). In the following section, we provide a brief overview of major findings in the AISB literature.

Several structured professional judgment risk and needs measures have been created, encompassing knowledge about risk factors for adolescent sexual recidivism. Those most frequently used (McGrath, Cumming, Burchard, Zeoli, & Ellerby, 2010) and researched include the Estimate of Risk of Adolescent Sexual Offense Recidivism (ERASOR) (Worling & Curwen, 2001) and the Juvenile Sex Offender Assessment Protocol–II (J-SOAP-II) (Prentky & Righthand, 2003). Research findings regarding the predictive accuracy of these instruments have been inconsistent; perhaps, at least in part, due to methodological constraints such as small sample sizes and samples of convenience (Viljoen, Mordell, & Beneteau, 2012). By aggregating the results of risk assessment studies investigating instruments used with AISB in a meta-analysis, Viljoen et al. were able to control for some of the methodological problems in individual studies and analyze the utility of the tools in a large sample of 6,196 individuals. Viljoen et al. reported that the predictive accuracy of these instruments was better than what was found for individual risk factors or nonsex-offense-specific risk assessment tools. The evidence regarding adolescent risk factors and assessment tools is not as broad and deep as it is for adults who have offended sexually, but including one or more of these validated risk measures for adolescents as part of an assessment is better than relying on unstructured clinical judgment alone (Viljoen et al.). Further, as Viljoen and her colleagues noted, measures that include dynamic factors may be most useful for identifying treatment targets and facilitating risk management and successful treatment outcomes.

Few attempts have been made to develop, and especially to test, protective-factor assessment scales with AISB. Bremer (2006) developed the Protective Factors Scale (PFS) to assess personal, family, and community assets that support positive behavior and pro-social development, including sexual behavior. Bremer (2006) suggested that the PFS could facilitate appropriate interventions that, in turn, could promote treatment progress as well as community safety when used in conjunction with the ERASOR (Worling & Curwen, 2001), which focuses on risk factors associated with sexual offending. The utility of the Protective Factors Scale for facilitating treatment and reducing sexual recidivism has not been evaluated empirically. More recently, Worling (2013) noted the dearth of research regarding strengths and protective factors and desistance from sexual offending, and developed the Desistence for Adolescents who Sexually Harm (DASH-13). In his monograph on the DASH-13, Worling reported that research on the psychometric properties and validity of the DASH-13 is underway.

A notable study (Griffin, Beech, Print, Bradshaw, & Quayle, 2008) regarding AISB provides support for Bremer's (2006) assessment model of integrating risk and protective factors to identify relevant treatment targets and guide effective interventions. In this study, the authors describe the development of the "draft" AIM-2, a holistic research-based structured assessment guide designed for males, ages 12 through 18 years, who have sexually abused others. The AIM-2 includes 75 static and dynamic individual, family or caregiver, and environmental factors that are scored as "concerns" (risk factors) or "strengths" (protective factors) and are categorized as low, medium, or high on each domain.

The predictive validity of the AIM-2 was tested with a randomly selected sample of 70 adolescents who were followed for a minimum of two years, with an average follow-up of six years. Findings indicated 10 percent, or seven adolescents, committed a new sexual offense. All of the sexual recidivists had high concern ratings (i.e., risk factors) and low strengths (i.e., protective factors). Further, subjects with high concern ratings but also high protective ratings were less likely to reoffend than those with similar concern ratings but few strengths, suggesting that the cumulative effect of multiple protective factors may reduce the likelihood of repeat offending.

Although protective factors and nonsexual reoffending by youths who have committed a range of nonviolent or violent offenses have received greater research attention than studies of AISB, this literature also is limited. A review of this literature also is beyond the scope of this book; however, the *Structured Assessment of Violence Risk in Youth* (SAVRY; Borum, Bartel, & Forth, 2002) is noteworthy for several reasons. The SAVRY was developed to assess risk factors associated with any kind of violent offending, including sexual reoffending (Borum, Bartel, & Forth, 2002). It is similar to the AIM-2 in that it has integrated six protective factors along with risk factors into a scale designed to facilitate structured clinical judgments about repeat violent offending and to facilitate effective interventions. The SAVRY protective factors are individual and environmental factors that generally are considered inconsistent with antisocial orientations: pro-social involvement, social support, strong attachment bonds, a positive attitude toward authority and intervention, commitment to school or work, and a resilient personality.

The SAVRY has been the focus of predictive validity studies and has demonstrated a positive association with future violent behavior (e.g., McGowan, Horn, & Mellott, 2011; Meyers & Schmidt, 2008; Vincent, Chapman, & Cook, 2011). Further, in a study of AISB, Viljoen et al. (2008) found the SAVRY was predictive of serious nonsexual violent recidivism, although its accuracy was better with older adolescents. It was not predictive of sexual reoffending, however. Although, the SAVRY protective items were not associated with reoffending of any kind following discharge from the treatment program, they were weakly to moderately related to nonsexual aggression during treatment, which suggests they are relevant targets of intervention. Recently, Spice et al. (2013) also did not find any SAVRY risk or protective items associated with sexual reoffending. The sample in this study, however, appears to be primarily the same as Viljoen et al.'s, although the sample size was increased by 24 adolescents.

In sum, this brief review of AISB risk and needs assessment measures reflects the importance of ongoing, methodologically sound research on risk and protective factors and assessment scales. Such research can improve risk and needs assessment by identifying and integrating individual and ecological validated-risk and protective factors and related measures that may help prioritize cases for treatment and supervision, titrate intervention intensity to risks and needs, and maximize the efficient and effective use of limited resources.

5 Effective Interventions

Introduction

Treatment participation has been positively associated with reducing the likelihood of sexual reoffending (Heilbrun et al., 2005). In their meta-analysis, Heilbrun and colleagues explored the relationship between participating in any type of treatment that had reducing sexual recidivism as its goal. Similarly, Hanson et al. (2009) conducted a meta-analysis of sex-offense-specific treatment outcome studies for adults (19 studies) and juveniles (4 studies) who had offended sexually. They found significantly lower sexual and general recidivism rates for those who had completed their treatment program compared with those who had no treatment, an alternative treatment, or less treatment. Large meta-analytic findings also have found that participation in therapeutic interventions reduces general delinquency (Lipsey, 2009).

In 2008, the Safer Society Foundation (SSF) conducted its ninth survey of North American juvenile and adult sex-offense-specific interventions (McGrath et al., 2010). Respondents to the SSF survey provided information on 1,379 treatment programs representing all 50 states, the District of Columbia, and nine Canadian provinces. This survey provides a snapshot of current treatment targets identified by treatment programs as therapeutic goals and objectives, which are summarized within the table in appendix B.

While the SSF Survey findings suggested many programs do appear to be using intervention strategies associated with effective interventions, such as cognitive-behavioral strategies, as McGrath et al. (2010) observed, some of the most commonly reported treatment targets have little or no empirical support as risk factors for sexual reoffending. Examples of these treatment targets include denial or minimization of the sexual offense, poor victim empathy, low self-esteem, general psychological problems, and experiencing sexual abuse as a child. While such factors may not be criminogenic needs, they may have relevance as responsivity needs, however. McGrath et al. (2010) also found that some empirically supported dynamic risk factors receive limited attention by treatment programs. For example, they noted a relatively small percentage of programs reported addressing well-supported criminogenic needs, such as appropriately managing sexual arousal and offense-supportive attitudes and beliefs.

As pointed out in the Risk, Need, and Responsivity Principles section of chapter 1 of this book, research indicates that service delivery and intervention intensity should be matched to risk level, such that persons with the most individual and socio-ecological risk factors associated with recidivism, and the fewest protective factors, receive the most intensive service delivery and treatment (e.g., Andrews & Bonta, 2010; Hanson et al., 2009). In contrast, individuals with few criminogenic needs may only require basic supervision and limited interventions, or even no treatment at all. In addition, also consistent with research and the RNR model, individuals who are low on sexual criminogenic needs (excessive sexual drive, atypical sexual interests, sexual preoccupation) but high on nonsexual risk factors may benefit the most from general delinquency interventions.

Although few studies have investigated treatment effectiveness with AISB, existing findings are encouraging (e.g., Fanniff & Becker, 2006; Heilbrun et al., 2005). Like adult sexual recidivism studies, this area of research is fraught with methodological challenges and limitations (see Reitzel & Carbonell, 2006). For example, studies frequently use weak experimental designs and employ small, convenience samples. There is heterogeneity in the handling of the effects of treatment dropouts or refusers. In addition, variations in outcome measures continue to hamper treatment-evaluation research. A well-designed study of recidivism among adults who have sexually offended (e.g., Marques, Wiederanders, Day, Nelson, & van Ommeren, 2005) also did not show positive treatment effects, indicating that caution is needed before confidently concluding that sex-offense-specific treatment is effective (see Seto et al., 2008). Nonetheless, better-controlled research suggests intervention with AISB can be effective, especially when it is matched to individual, family, and socio-ecological risk and protective factors and to treatment needs.

Although a full review of outcome studies is beyond the scope of this paper, relevant findings, recent studies, and meta-analytic reviews are summarized briefly below. While not a complete listing, readers may find the following individual studies and literature reviews of interest: Becker and Hunter (1997); Bourke and Donohue (1996); Efta-Breitbach and Freeman (2004); Fanniff and Becker (2006); Hunter and Figueredo (1999); Reitzel and Carbonell (2006); Righthand and Welch (2001, 2004); Walker et al. (2004); Worling and Langton (2012); and Zimring (2004).

Meta-Analytic Reviews Focusing Primarily on Adults Who Offended Sexually

Historically, intervention efforts with AISB were based upon what was known at the time regarding sex-offense-specific treatment with adults (Chaffin & Bonner, 1998). Some meta-analytical reviews have suggested that sex-offense-specific treatment was effective. For example, in their study of 43 treatment programs, including 4 studies of AISB, Hanson et al. (2002) found nearly a 5 percent difference in sexual recidivism rates between individuals who completed sex-offense-specific treatment and those who did not. Cognitive-behavioral and systemic interventions were associated with significant reductions in sexual and nonsexual reoffending, whereas older forms of treatment offered prior to 1980 were not.

More recently, Schmucker and Lösel (2008) conducted a more extensive meta-analysis. Most studies examined adults with sex offenses but seven focused on AISB. Most studies found that treatment was positively associated with reduced re-offense rates. The meta-analytic findings indicated an 11 percent versus 18 percent difference in sexual recidivism between those who received treatment and those who did not, suggesting sexual recidivism was reduced by approximately a third. Similar results were found for nonsexual recidivism. Cognitive-behavioral, behavioral, and hormonal-treatment interventions, compared with other treatments, had more positive treatment effects.

In another recent meta-analysis that included 19 investigations of treatment outcomes with adults who offended sexually as well as 4 studies of AISB, Hanson et al. (2009) found an 11 percent versus 19 percent difference in sexual recidivism between those who received treatment and the comparison group. Lower rates of nonsexual recidivism also were found in the treatment group. Of special interest, Hanson et al. (2009) investigated the extent to which treatment programs adhered to the risk, need, and responsivity principles of effective correctional intervention (Andrews & Bonta, 2010). Hanson and his colleagues found significantly lower rates of sexual and nonsexual recidivism from programs that adhered more closely to RNR principles. This finding adds to the growing research support for the principles of effective correctional interventions with both adolescents and adults who have engaged in illegal behavior (e.g., Andrews & Bonta, 2010; Hawkins et al., 1998; Lipsey, 1995; Lipsey, 1999; Marlowe, Festinger, Lee, Dugosh, & Benasutti, 2006; Pealer & Latessa, 2004).

While it is important not to ignore findings from studies that focus primarily on adults who have offended sexually, it is also important not to automatically apply these findings to AISB. As noted earlier in chapter 1, AISB differ in meaningful ways from adults who commit sexual offenses. It is essential to keep in mind that the cognitive, social-emotional, and character development of adolescents is still in flux, and to tailor interventions accordingly.

Meta-Analytic Findings Focusing on Children with Sexual Behavior Problems

Factors associated with puberty, adolescence, and life experiences may distinguish adolescents from children in meaningful ways. Yet, older children and younger adolescents may have much in common; both are youths, not adults. Thus, findings regarding treatment outcomes for children with sexual behavior problems are important to consider as well. St. Armand, Parks, and Silovsky (2008) conducted a meta-analysis of treatment outcomes for children ages 3–12 with sexual behavior problems. Study findings revealed significant reductions in sexual and nonsexual behavior problems. When treatment components were examined more closely, improvements were associated with caregiver-focused interventions, that is, facilitating positive parenting and behavior management skills, rules about sexual behavior, sex education, and abuse prevention skills, as well as treatment increasing self-control skills in children

Additionally, a long-term follow-up study of children with sexual behavior problems provides further support for cognitive-behavioral treatment of children with sexual behavior problems. Carpentier, Silovsky, and Chaffin (2006) examined criminal-offense and child-welfare records of children who had been randomized to a brief outpatient child and caregiver cognitive-behavioral treatment or a play-therapy model. This 10-year follow-up found only 2 percent of the youths who had been in the cognitive-behavioral treatment had offended sexually compared with 11 percent for those in the control group. These low rates of future sexual offending combined with the St. Armand et al. (2008) meta-analysis provide strong support for these effective treatment intervention models with children who have had sexual behavior problems, as well as the importance of involving caregivers in treatment.

Meta-Analytic Findings Involving Adolescents with Illegal Sexual Behavior

Meta-analyses of treatment outcome with AISB suggest that treatment may reduce the likelihood of sexual recidivism. Walker, McGovern, Poey, and Otis (2004) appear to be the first researchers to have conducted a meta-analysis of AISB. Their study included 10 published and unpublished studies. Findings indicated that all of the treatments in their meta-analysis were positively associated with reduced sexual recidivism. Cognitive-behavioral therapy had the strongest effects.

Reitzel and Carbonell (2006) conducted a meta-analysis of nine published and unpublished studies and found an almost 11 percent difference in sexual recidivism rates between AISB who completed a sex-offense-specific treatment program (7 percent) and those receiving no treatment (19 percent). For every 43 treatment participants who recidivated sexually, 100 non-completers reoffended sexually. Comparisons regarding treatment modality were not significant. Reitzel and Carbonell urged caution when interpreting these meta-analytic findings. Like other researchers, they cited an array of methodological limitations, such as the relatively small number of studies, small sample sizes, varying follow-up periods, and divergent strategies for controlling for treatment dropouts.

Heilbrun et al. (2005) identified nine published studies for their meta-analysis focusing on risk factors and needs of AISB. They found that too few of the studies provided sufficient information about the specific types of treatment offered. Therefore, they created a composite "intervention" item that included studies that provided information about outcomes from any type of treatment that had reducing sexual recidivism as a goal. This intervention variable was significantly related to sexual recidivism, suggesting that treatment efforts with AISB were effective at reducing sexual recidivism.

Promising Treatment Models

Multisystemic therapy (MST) for problematic sexual behavior is the only intervention with strong empirical support for reducing sexual offending through randomized clinical trials (Pullman & Seto, 2012). Initially MST was designed to intervene with youths who engaged in serious and chronic delinquency. Interventions were designed to effect positive, long-term changes in adolescent antisocial behavior by targeting the youth's socio-ecological context, that is, his family, neighborhood, school, and community. Henggeler et al. (1998) noted the focus of treatment is not only, or even primarily, the adolescent. By using cognitive-behavioral, social-learning and family-systems methods, MST works to facilitate caregivers' abilities to intervene with their children more effectively in their natural environment; for example, therapy sessions often take place at home or at school rather than in an office.

MST outcome research includes multiple randomized clinical trials (though only a few have been independent of the MST developers) (Henggeler et al., 1998). Curtis et al. (2004) conducted a meta-analysis of 11 MST outcome studies. The sample included 708 youths but only one study of 16 AISB. Seventy percent of the youths and families who received MST did better than those who received alternative treatments. Youths and family members who received MST evidenced improved emotional and behavioral functioning, better parent–child relationships, and decreases in negative peer association, aggression toward peers, and criminal behavior. Improvements in family relations exceeded improvements in individual youths or their peer relations. The importance of implementation fidelity (i.e., adherence to the treatment model) was indicated because programs with higher fidelity produced better outcomes.

Although not all studies (e.g., Littell, Popa, & Forsythe, 2005) have replicated these positive MST findings, differing treatment methodologies may have accounted for disparate findings (Henggeler et al., 2006; Ogden & Hagen, 2006). Leschied and Cunningham (2002) also did not replicate findings that MST was more effective than treatment as usual in their randomized treatment study. They described the MST treatment as implemented with fidelity to the MST model. When discussing their findings, they pointed out MST may not be more effective than other interventions *when* the alternative treatments are *effective* interventions. This explanation is consistent with Lipsey's (2009) meta-analytic finding regarding therapeutic interventions for juvenile delinquency, which found that "generic" interventions provided to those with the highest risk to reoffend (consistent with the risk principle, as discussed previously) by well-trained and supervised staff who monitor progress and program fidelity are as effective as branded interventions such as MST. (Lipsey noted that his meta-analytic review did not provide sufficient data for testing the need and responsivity principles because research studies typically do not provide sufficient information about the targets of intervention or the strategies that may be used to enhance treatment effectiveness.)

As discussed below, results from a recent study of MST for problematic sexual behavior (MST-PSB), not included in the above meta-analytic reviews, is encouraging as well. MST-PSB is the name given to the MST model that was adapted specifically for AISB. As noted on the MST Services website, the adaptation includes addressing denial by the youth and family about the problematic sexual behavior, assessing and focusing on aspects of the youth's environment that contribute to the sexual offending, developing individualized and practical safety plans for the youth and family, and helping caregivers provide clear direction and support that can help the youth develop healthy peer relationships as well as support networks for the family (Multisystemic Therapy Services, Inc., n.d).

Of note, MST-PSB is the only treatment approach specifically for AISB that has been empirically validated by randomized controlled studies. Sample sizes were small in the first two trials (16 in Borduin et al., 1990, and 48 in Borduin et al., 2009), and did not involve comparison to a current treatment approach. The recent MST-PSB clinical trial referenced above has a much larger sample, with 127 AISB randomized to MST-PSB or current treatment for AISB provided as usual (Letourneau et al., 2009). Preliminary findings are promising and consistent with the earlier research. When compared with the usual community-based services, MST-PSB produced greater improvements in family and peer relations and academic performance and evidenced greater reductions in substance use, criminal behavior, and problematic sexual behavior (Henggeler et al., 2009; Letourneau et al., 2009). At the time the initial findings were presented, sexual recidivism was not considered a useful indicator of the treatment outcome because only one youth in the entire sample had reoffended at the 12-month mark. Instead, the researchers assessed problematic sexual behavior by adolescent and parent reports on two scales of the Adolescent Clinical Sexual Behavior Inventory (ACSBI; Friedrich, Lysne, Sim, & Shamos, 2004). One measure was the "deviant" sexual interests subscale that includes items such as owning pornography, use of phone-sex lines, and voyeurism, and the other was the sexual risk/misuse subscale that assesses overt sexual behaviors such as having unprotected sex, being sexually used by others, and pushing others into having sex. The validity of the ACSBI as an indicator of sex-offending risk, however, has not been demonstrated (Hecker, 2014). The ACSBI findings do suggest MST-PSB was useful for promoting healthier sexual behavior overall. As the authors stated, additional follow-up studies are necessary to better evaluate MST-PSB's effectiveness at reducing sexual recidivism, and these studies are underway (Letourneau et al., 2009).

Another outpatient treatment model that has shown promise is the Sexual Abuse: Family Education and Treatment (SAFE-T) Program in Toronto. A 10-year follow-up evaluation of the SAFE-T program (Worling, Litteljohn, & Bookalam, 2010), too recent to be included in the meta-analyses discussed above, provides additional support for community-based sex-offense-specific treatments that are assessment-driven and individually tailored to meet each youth's and his or her family's risks and treatment needs. The SAFE-T program is clinic-based and less treatment-intensive than the home-based MST model. Like MST, however, it involves caregivers.

In their research, Worling and colleagues (2010) followed 58 adolescents (53 males and 5 females) who participated in at least 10 months of specialized sex-offense-specific treatment and 90 youths who were assessed only, refused treatment, or dropped out prior to 12 months of treatment. Overall, 67 percent of the comparison group in Worling et al.'s (2010) study received some treatment, although the details and duration were unknown. The specialized sex-offense-specific treatment typically involved concurrent group, individual, and family therapy with interventions tailored to individual strengths, risk factors, and treatment needs. The adolescents were followed for 12 to 20 years. Recidivism rates for youths in the specialized treatment group were 9 percent for sexual recidivism and 21 percent for the comparison group; 22 percent for violent nonsexual recidivism for the specialized treatment group and 39 percent for the comparison group; and 28 percent for nonviolent, nonsexual recidivism and 52 percent for the comparison group. These positive findings are encouraging and suggest that not all adolescents with AISB require the treatment intensity of the MST model.

Yet, because the Worling et al. (2010) study was not a randomized trial, it is unknown whether the increased recidivism of the comparison group may have been due, at least in part, to characteristics of the teens or their families. We would expect adolescents who refuse or drop out of treatment to differ in their motivation to change, their antisocial attitudes and beliefs, their ability to follow rules, and other factors. Of note, adult sex-offense-treatment outcome evaluations have shown that individuals who refuse or drop out of treatment are at greater risk of recidivism than those who willingly participate in treatment (Hanson et al., 2002).

Not all AISB outcome studies have demonstrated positive outcomes for sex-offense-specific interventions. For example, Lab, Shields, and Schondel (1993) compared sex-offense-specific treatment with treatment provided for general delinquency. The researchers found low recidivism rates for both groups. Although the low base rate hampers the study's ability to demonstrate differences between groups, these findings also may suggest that an initial assessment of the AISB (see the typology section in the introduction) is critical in order to plan effective intervention; in line with the risk principle of effective intervention, not all AISB require specialized sex-offense-specific treatment.

One treatment model, Multidimensional Treatment Foster Care (MTFC), is similar to MST in that it provides multisystemic interventions to youths with significant antisocial behaviors. Although not a sex-offense-specific treatment model, AISB may be accepted for MTFC when appropriate. MTFC provides intensive interventions for youths and treatment foster families while also working with the family to which the youth will return following placement. MTFC has been shown to be effective for youths with serious delinquency and violence in multiple research studies (e.g., Chamberlain et al. 2007; Chamberlain & Reid, 1998; Eddy, Whaley, & Chamberlain, 2004), including randomized trials. It is noteworthy that as many as 20 percent of the adolescents in the Chamberlain and Reid MTFC study had histories of sex offending as well as nonsexual delinquency.[1]

MTFC or other delinquency interventions may be appropriate in cases that include illegal sexual behavior or sexual behavior problems, but where a general pattern of delinquent behavior is the primary presenting problem. General delinquency interventions would be particularly useful for AISB who fall in the early/persistent delinquency group discussed earlier. As the RNR model delineates, assessment-driven interventions that match evidence-based dynamic individual and family risk and protective factors with well-implemented, individualized, clinical interventions may be important for facilitating positive outcomes.[2]

---

1 Personal communication to first author from Patricia Chamberlain, May 1, 2006.
2 See http://www.blueprintsprograms.com/about.php for further information about effective interventions for prevention violence and delinquency; also see SAMHSA's National Registry of Evidence-Based Programs and Practices (NREPP) for information about substance abuse and mental health interventions: http://www.nrepp.samhsa.gov and the California Evidence-Based Clearinghouse for Child Welfare: http://www.cebc4cw.org.

Possible Barriers to Treatment

As noted in chapter 3, potential barriers to successfully engaging clients include not recognizing and addressing individual learning styles, mental health challenges, and cultural factors. Examples of other potential barriers include the parents' degree of believing or denying allegations of sexual-offending behavior (Frey, 1995; Rich, 2003; Stevenson, Castillo, & Sefarbi, 1989), parents' own victimization histories (New, Stevenson, & Skuse, 1999), as well as the divided loyalties some parents might experience in cases of sibling incest. Practical obstacles must be addressed as well, such as work schedules, parenting responsibilities toward other children, transportation, and scheduling difficulties. These challenges can make it difficult for family members to participate in treatment sessions as well as to serve as supports, supervisors, and positive role models.

Treatment Engagement and Completion

Research findings (Seabloom, Seabloom, Seabloom, Barron, & Hendrickson, 2003) suggest that failing to complete treatment or not satisfactorily completing treatment goals are associated with sexual recidivism and higher rates of nonsexual reoffending. These findings highlight the importance of addressing treatment refusers and dropouts when evaluating treatment outcomes (cf. Worling et al., 2010). Studies with adults have yielded similar findings (e.g., Hanson et al., 2002; Marques et al., 2005; Seager, Jellicoe, & Dhaliwal, 2004). Engaging and maintaining adolescents in treatment can be challenging. For example, Rasmussen (1999) found over half of the participants in her primarily community outpatient sample completed their recommended treatment, one-third failed to complete treatment once they began, and the rest either did not follow through or were not recommended for treatment. Kraemer, Salisbury, and Spielman (1998) reported that completion rates for juvenile residential sex-offense-specific programs in Minnesota ranged from 30 percent to 50 percent. Their study suggested that older age and impulsivity were associated with treatment dropout. Similarly, Hunter and Figueredo (1999) found that attrition from treatment during the first year was as high as 50 percent. Twenty percent of these youths ended treatment owing to reasons that were probably unrelated to their attitudes or behavior (e.g., family relocation), but 33 percent were expelled from the program as "treatment failures." Few were expelled for new sexual (4.9 percent) or nonsexual offenses (6.6 percent); treatment expulsion was due to poor attendance or noncompliance with treatment directives. Those who were most noncompliant were described as more sexually maladjusted (as measured by the Multiphasic Sex Inventory; Nichols & Molinder, 1984), and were possibly at greater risk of sexual offending.

Schram et al. (1991) found that most AISB terminated treatment as soon as their sentence or court order ended. Only 29 percent of their sample was considered to have completed treatment, yet only 12 percent were arrested for a new sexual offense. Nonsexual reoffending was more likely (51 percent), but 37 percent were not rearrested for any kind of new offense. As Schram et al. noted, therapists may significantly overestimate the risk of sexual recidivism (57 percent were considered "at risk" of sexual recidivism and an additional 10 percent were considered "dangerous"), and may attempt to keep AISB in treatment longer than necessary. Given that many AISB reoffended nonsexually, treatment providers also may not focus sufficiently on general delinquency risk factors (see Quinsey, Skilling, Lalumière, & Craig, 2004).

High treatment attrition rates are concerning. The attrition rates suggest that positive treatment outcomes are, at least in part, due to treatment participation by more motivated clients. Adolescents who are impulsive or noncompliant may be more challenging to engage in treatment, but they may be among those who need treatment most. Denying or minimizing sexual offending frequently is considered an obstacle to treatment participation (McGrath et al., 2010). Some clinicians believe adversarial techniques such as polygraph examinations or pressure to accept responsibility as a condition of treatment participation are necessary to foster disclosures of offending behavior and other thoughts, fantasies, or behaviors that are potentially problematic (e.g., see Chaffin, 2008; 2010). Harsh strategies can be counter-therapeutic or even harmful as they may inhibit or discourage therapeutic rapport and motivation to change.

Therapist characteristics and interventions that help adolescents develop a sense of self-efficacy, an internal locus of control, and increased social responsibility are likely to be more effective for helping youths accept increasing responsibility for their behavior and facilitating treatment engagement, participation, and progress (cf. Marshall, Thornton, Marshall, Fernandez, & Mann, 2001). In the process, adolescents may acknowledge previous sexually abusive behavior as a natural progression in becoming a more responsible person.

As noted by McGrath et al.'s (2010) Safer Society survey, although treatment providers appeared to be aware of the importance of motivation and therapeutic engagement for promoting positive outcomes, only half of adolescent programs reported utilizing strategies such as motivational interviewing. Treatment motivation can be enhanced by the therapist showing respect to the client, ignoring or not engaging in discussions that involve denying or minimizing the offending, offering hope with therapy, and collaborating with clients and helping them identify relevant, specific, and achievable treatment goals (e.g., Lambie & McCarthy, 2004). Effective treatment engagement strategies can enhance treatment participation, retention, and completion. The necessity of engaging clients in ways that are motivating and encouraging, rather than overfocusing on details of the sex offenses in ways that may be unnecessarily shaming, cannot be overstated (Jenkins, 2006). We can use motivational interviewing and engagement strategies to foster positive change and pro-social development (e.g., O'Reilly, Morrison, Sheerin, & Carr, 2001).

Caregiver Engagement

Given that adolescents are still minors and are usually still dependent on caregivers' emotional and economic support, it is unsurprising that caregiver involvement in a youth's treatment is important. As Worling and Långström (2003) found, programs that combined offense-specific treatment with strong family involvement demonstrated less sexual and nonsexual recidivism than other programs. Similarly, the MST-PSB model emphasizes the role of caregiver involvement and capacity to supervise and intervene with the youth.

Recent research has shown that families who participated in a community-based adolescent sex-offense-specific treatment program indicated improved communication capabilities and parent–child relationships, fewer conflicts between family members, and a more harmonious home environment (Henggeler et al., 2009; Thornton et al., 2008).

In a study involving intrafamilial sexual abuse by siblings, Thornton et al. (2008) found that, following interventions, parents reported having more confidence in their parenting skills and a greater understanding of how their behavior influenced overall family functioning. Their adolescents reported increased self-control, improved emotional regulation, and better social skills; improvements were more likely when an adolescent had at least one parent participate and engage in therapy with them. As Henggeler et al. (2009) have noted, such changes in caregiver and family functioning can be important mediators of positive, lasting changes in the behavior and lives of their children.

6 Summary and Discussion

Effective interventions with AISB are developmentally appropriate, assessment-driven, and well implemented. They target dynamic risk and protective factors that are empirically associated with repeated sexual and nonsexual offending. To be most useful, assessments, case planning, and interventions are holistic and include a socio-ecological focus that considers not only the adolescent, but caregivers, peers, and other social influences.

Assessment

Evidence-based, offense-specific needs assessments are an essential component of interventions with AISB. They are necessary for planning and implementing appropriate interventions, monitoring progress, and assessing timely treatment completion or discharge from termination of additional interventions. In keeping with the RNR principles of effective intervention, the intensity of intervention should be titrated to ensure that those who present with the most risks and fewest protective factors receive the most intensive services and supports. Further, intervention should focus on dynamic risk and protective factors that are empirically associated with reducing the likelihood of reoffending. High-quality assessments of risk and protective factors associated with offending are needed, not only for guiding effective treatment interventions, but also for prioritizing cases and facilitating other decisions such as home, community, or residential placement, sentencing, and supervision conditions.

Effective interventions involve careful consideration of factors that may affect treatment responsiveness. Such factors include the adolescent's and caregiver's learning style, possible co-occurring disorders, motivation for positive change, cultural values and beliefs, practical obstacles, and so forth. Although these factors may not be empirically associated with reoffending, they can be central to the adolescent's or his family's abilities to respond positively to interventions.

As reviewed in this book, a number of dynamic criminogenic needs have been identified in the adult sexual recidivism and AISB literatures. As described in the table in appendix A and in chapter 2, these include problems with *sexuality*, such as atypical sexual interests, excessive sexual drive, pro-sex-offending attitudes, and inadequate sexual self-regulation; *social bonds and orientation* such as antisocial attitudes and beliefs, noncompliance with rules, and negative peer associations; *general self-regulation* difficulties, such as emotional dysregulation and impulsive behaviors; deficits in *social competence*, including conflicts in interpersonal relationships and social isolation; and inadequate *socio-ecological supports*, such as inconsistent caregiving, monitoring, and support.

Dynamic protective factors that may reduce the risk of sexual reoffending have received limited research attention thus far. We have noted some studies that have described factors associated with desistance from repeat offending, and research suggests that the presence of strengths or protective factors may mitigate or buffer the negative effects of risk factors and concerns (e.g., Griffin et al., 2008).

Many of these criminogenic needs are well established in the treatment of juvenile delinquency, suggesting important commonalities in assessment and treatment approaches (see Pullman & Seto, 2012). Assessments must specifically identify relevant risk and protective factors and recommend appropriate evidence-based interventions, such as cognitive-behavioral and socio-ecological interventions to reduce recidivism risk.

Treatment

In this book, we utilized a potentially useful heuristic for conceptualizing the criminogenic factors and intervention needs of these adolescents that is based upon early theories (Becker & Kaplan, 1988; O'Brien & Bera, 1986) and more recent research findings (e.g., Hunter, 2006; Hunter et al., 2004; Way & Urbaniak, 2008). The conceptualization involves four groups: (1) *situational*; (2) *early onset or serious delinquency*; (3) *atypical sexual interests/preoccupation*; and (4) *both serious delinquency and atypical sexual interests*.

These four groups can be created by crossing the two major risk dimensions identified in the sexual-offending literature, one having to do with antisocial propensities and the other to do with atypical sexual interests and sexual preoccupation (Hanson & Bussiere, 1998; Hanson & Morton-Bourgon, 2005).

Adolescents who have few risk factors on both the atypical sexual interests/drive and early onset or serious delinquency dimensions are most likely situational and transitory in their offending and least likely to reoffend. These adolescents may not require treatment, or may require only limited treatment once they are identified. Some of them may have been aware of the wrongfulness of their behavior and even stopped on their own, before being caught and sanctioned informally or formally. In contrast, adolescents who are high in antisocial tendencies, but low in atypical sexual interests or sexual preoccupation, may benefit most from effective general delinquency interventions like MST, MTFC, or a generic intervention that is evidence-based and follows RNR principles. Such interventions would include addressing antisocial attitudes and beliefs associated with sex offending, as well as other illegal behaviors, along with promoting pro-social orientations that include valuing age-appropriate, consensual, and legal intimate relationships.

Adolescents who are low in antisocial tendencies but high in atypical sexual interests/drive are relatively few in number, but they are at greater risk of committing another sexual offense than situational or delinquent AISB. Thus, they require interventions that specifically focus on their sexual interests and sexual self-regulation. Similarly, the fourth group is also small in number, but AISB in this group pose the greatest concern for both sexual and nonsexual offending because they have many risk factors from both the *sexual* and *antisocial* risk dimensions. These adolescents likely will require the most intensive interventions combining effective techniques from general-delinquency treatment and sex-offense-specific treatment.

Logically and empirically, treatment of adolescent sexual offending can draw a great deal from empirically supported interventions for juvenile delinquency. The exception is in the sexual domain, where service providers need to assess sexual interests and behaviors and treatment needs to address sexual interests and self-regulation skills for some AISB. The evidence regarding treatment approaches and outcomes is becoming clearer (cf. Worling, 2012). For example, family involvement is a very important component of effective treatment with AISB. Efforts to positively engage family members should be a major focus of interventions. When family members are not available, appropriate, or willing to be involved, alternative positive and supportive caregivers or other appropriate adults may be engaged in treatment and as community supports and mentors whenever possible.

The importance of family and community-involved interventions is demonstrated by MST, which emphasizes ecologically valid and practical interventions for adolescents and their families. An adapted version, MST-PSB, remains the only treatment approach for AISB that is supported by the most rigorous outcome-evaluation design, which involves the randomized clinical trial.

MST-PSB is not available everywhere, however, and although it may be cost-effective (Aos, Phipps, Barnoski, & Lieb, 2001), especially when used with adolescents who require intensive treatment and are at risk of residential or correctional placement, the costs of maintaining high standards of training and ensuring fidelity are high. Further, the MST-PSB model has not been empirically validated with some populations. For example, adolescents with autism spectrum disorders (ASD) may be excluded from MST-PSB. The newly developed MST for disruptive behavior problems in youths with autism spectrum disorders reflects the perceived need for a more specialized intervention with this population (Wagner et al., 2013).

Available research suggests additional approaches also may be effective, especially when they include increasing caregiver monitoring and involvement. As Lipsey's (2009) meta-analysis showed, effective interventions depend less on the "brand" than on how well the intervention is implemented. Lipsey found that therapeutic interventions provided by well-trained and supervised staff that monitored progress and made adaptations to ensure high-quality implementation and positive outcomes effectively reduced recidivism among juveniles considered at high risk for reoffending.

Lastly, with the exception of MST, a general-delinquency intervention now adapted for juveniles with problematic sexual behavior (e.g., Borduin et al., 2009), treatment-outcome research designs have not randomly assigned adolescents to treatment and control groups, which is the best method to control for extraneous factors that can confound group comparisons. More rigorously designed treatment evaluation studies are needed.

Future Research

Future research is needed to better identify dynamic risk and protective factors and improve offense-specific needs-assessment measures for adolescents who sexually offend. Given that available measures have only limited evidence of predictive validity so far, there will likely be value in distinguishing between long-term risk to offend (best predicted by static or historical factors such as age and criminal history) (e.g., Ralston & Epperson, 2013), and shorter-term dynamic risk and protective factors. Further work is also needed on the best ways to assess atypical sexual interests, given concerns about the potential impact (and limited availability) of phallometric testing.

Finally, as has been increasingly stressed (e.g., Association for the Treatment of Sexual Abusers, 2012), and emphasized in this book as well, adolescents are not adults. We must keep in mind that the cognitive and social-emotional skills and character of adolescents are still developing (see chapter 1). Adolescent brain development continues until the early or mid-twenties. Developmental research on this "emerging adulthood" phase (Arnett, 2010) is just beginning. Most studies of adolescents include youth up to age 18 or 21, as some states keep youth who have sexually offended prior to 18 in their juvenile system until age 21.

The question remains, are these young adults more like AISB or like adults with sex offenses? Are adolescent or adult risk assessment tools most accurate? Are adolescent treatment models and interventions most effective, or are those designed for adults best; or is something specifically designed for this age group likely to be most effective? These and other questions remain to be answered. Ongoing quality research, and thoughtful examination and application of those research findings, will continue to contribute to knowledge about how to protect children by effectively treating AISB.

Appendix A:
Criminogenic Treatment Targets: Summary Table

Sexuality 65
Social Bonds & Orientation 66
General Self-Regulation 67
Social Competence 68
Socio-Ecological Factors 69

Criminogenic Treatment Targets: Summary Table	
Sexuality	Sexual behaviors are expressions of interests, arousal, and drive.
Sexual interests	AISB may offend in spite of age-appropriate sexual interests. Atypical sexual interests are defined as uncommon and unusual sexual interests, arousal, and behavior. There is limited research with adolescents, but these studies indicate atypical sexual interests are related to increased rates of sexual reoffending and number of sexual victims. This may be more of issue for AISB who offend against young children, especially boys.
Sex drive and preoccupation	Research suggests some adolescents who offend sexually have higher rates of sexual preoccupation, compulsivity, and excessive sex drive than adolescents with nonsexual offenses. Though evidence is stronger for adults, research has shown a positive association between unusually high sex drive and excessive sexual preoccupation during adolescence and sexual recidivism.
Sexual self-regulation	Refers to using relevant information and skills to successfully manage sexual arousal appropriately and also satisfy sexual urges in healthy, non-abusive ways.
Attitudes and beliefs regarding sex and sex offending	Some AISB may have generally pro-social attitudes and beliefs about abusive sexual behavior, but justify their actions in spite of such beliefs. Others may have negative, hostile, and stereotypical views about women and sex or a preference for impersonal sex, while others may endorse offense-supportive attitudes about sex with children.

Criminogenic Treatment Targets: Summary Table (continued)

Social Bonds & Orientation	Social bonds and orientation refer to the extent to which an adolescent identifies with and subscribes to pro-social values, as compared with antisocial attitudes and beliefs, and generally behaves accordingly.
Antisocial orientation	This orientation encompasses antisocial traits such as impulsivity, substance abuse, chronic truancy or, if not in school, unemployment, and a history of rule violations. In more severe instances, it may include lifestyle instability and a callous disregard for the welfare of others. Research supports an association between antisociality (i.e., hostility) and sexual offending, and suggests it is an important risk factor for sexual recidivism. Additionally, an antisocial orientation increases the likelihood of adolescents being noncompliant with, and dropping out of, treatment.
Antisocial attitudes and beliefs	Criminal thinking involves values, perspectives, as well as emotional states that are self-centered, disregard the welfare of others, and view dishonesty, crime, and violence as justifiable and appropriate alternatives. Antisocial attitudes and beliefs may be transitory or entrenched and are not specific to sexual offending, but when present, interventions that address such attitudes and beliefs may help facilitate pro-social thinking and lifestyles that are incompatible with reoffending.
Peer associations	Negative peer associations, i.e., having peers who present an antisocial influence, are a strong predictor for the development and persistence of offending. Additionally, knowing a person who had offended sexually was associated with greater self-reported sexual violence, suggesting peer influence on sexual offending and/or co-offending.

Criminogenic Treatment Targets: Summary Table (continued)

General Self-Regulation	Self-regulation includes the ability to focus and concentrate effectively and successfully manage emotions and impulses in positive and healthy ways.
Problems with self-regulation	Problems with self-regulation include attentional and concentration difficulties, restlessness and hyperactivity, impulsive behavior, and risk taking. These deficits are associated with a wide range of challenges and have been strongly associated with sexual recidivism, and other types of reoffending.
Impulsivity	This is a personality trait describing the predisposition to act suddenly and without much forethought. There is some research that has demonstrated links between impulsivity and sexual offending. Conceivably, when provided with an opportunity to offend, one can act, perhaps impulsively and without consideration for the consequences of such behavior, and take advantage of the perceived opportunity.
School behavior problems	As discussed here, this domain does not focus primarily on the youth's intellectual and cognitive abilities, but is concerned with factors such as attention difficulties, impulsivity, and conduct problems. Academic and school experiences of adolescents who engage in sexually abusive behavior vary, but several studies have found academic difficulties related to sexual recidivism.
Substance abuse	Substance abuse may reflect poor self-regulation and contribute to other personal, family, and social problems. Studies have not identified substance abuse as a risk factor for sexual reoffending, but research has shown that AISB with fewer substance abuse problems were more likely to stop sexual reoffending than others.
Emotional self-regulation deficits	Effectively expressing emotions requires the ability to identify one's own feelings correctly, as well as those of others. Difficulty identifying, expressing, and coping with negative emotions may contribute to adolescents' violent behavior in general, and research has linked escalations in negative emotions with adolescent sex offending. It's important to remember, however, that acquiring emotional and self-regulation are developmental processes associated with brain development, which continues into young adulthood.

Criminogenic Treatment Targets: Summary Table (continued)

Social Competence	Social competence refers to the social, emotional, cognitive, and behavioral skills required to successfully develop and maintain productive relationships with others. Although the areas described here primarily focus on the adolescent's abilities to develop and maintain age-appropriate social and intimate relationships, social competence is important in multiple domains, such as school and vocational pursuits.
Social and intimate relationships	Refers to the types, quality, and sustainability of interpersonal relationships. AISB tend to have more heterosocial-skills deficits, general social-skills deficits, and other social problems than adolescents with nonsexual offenses.
	Little research has explored adolescent dating and intimate relationships; however, a significant association has been documented between recidivism rates and variables such as poor social skills, negative social influences, conflicts in intimate relationships, emotional identification with children, and loneliness.
Social isolation	Social isolation can be a result of geography, minimal access to transportation, or, for some, poor social skills and low self-esteem.
	Research has indicated that AISB have experienced greater social isolation than those who committed nonsexual crimes. However, findings from studies regarding the social relationships of AISB and recidivism rates have been mixed. Some studies have indicated that social-skills deficits resulting in the inability to develop age-appropriate peer and intimate relationships have been linked to sexual recidivism.
Emotional congruence with children	Emotional congruence with children typically involves an adolescent who identifies and feels most comfortable with children who are significantly younger than the adolescent as contrasted with age-appropriate peers. In such instances the adolescent prefers associating with children to meet interpersonal, emotional, and intimacy needs.
	Congruence with children has long been theorized to be a risk factor for child sexual abuse in adult-offending models, and a preference for associating with significantly younger children may be risk-relevant for adolescents as well.

Criminogenic Treatment Targets: Summary Table (continued)

Socio-Ecological Factors	Socio-ecological research has demonstrated the importance of parental/caregiver availability, monitoring, and support.
Family and caregivers	Caregiver conflict, rejection, or other dysfunction is associated with offending of different kinds, including sexual offending.
Additional adult supports	Pro-social community members can engage youth in positive activities and provide mentoring opportunities. Further, general delinquency research has found the beneficial impact of having a positive adult role model.
Community ties	Social isolation and "weak social ties" have been associated with both sexual and nonsexual offending. Adolescents with fewer negative peer associations and influences are less likely to recidivate. Adolescents who are positively engaged in school or who obtain stable employment have less recidivism.

Appendix B:
Treatment Targets for Adolescents with Illegal Sexual Behaviors: Information from The Safer Society 2009 Nationwide Survey[1]

---

[1] Adapted with permission from: McGrath, R. J., Cumming, G. F., Burchard, B. L., Zeoli, S., & Ellerby, L. (2010). *Current practices and trends in sexual abuser management: The Safer Society 2009 nationwide survey.* Brandon, VT: Safer Society Press.

Treatment Targets for Adolescents with Illegal Sexual Behaviors: Information from The Safer Society 2009 Nationwide Survey

	U.S. Community Programs		U.S. Residential Programs		Canada Community Programs	
	Male n = 272	Female n = 101	Male n = 95	Female n = 18	Male n = 15	Female n = 6
Arousal control	57.5	53.9	61.2	36.8	53.3	66.7
Emotional regulation	65.8	71.3	76.8	77.8	66.7	66.7
Family support networks	94.0	96.0	89.6	88.2	71.4	83.3
Intimacy/ relationship skills	86.8	85.1	87.4	66.7	86.7	100
Offense responsibility	88.2	86.1	93.7	72.2	86.7	66.7
Offense-supportive attitudes	51.8	55.4	45.3	44.4	53.3	66.7
Problem solving	86.0	83.2	90.5	94.4	86.7	100
Self-monitoring	54.0	49.5	57.9	55.6	60.0	66.7
Social-skills training	94.1	94.1	98.9	88.9	86.7	100
Victim awareness and empathy	92.6	93.1	94.7	94.4	93.3	100

Note: n = programs responding. Table shows percentage of programs incorporating core treatment components.

References

Abel, G. G., Jordan, A., Rouleau, J. L., Emerick, R., Barboza-Whitehead, S., & Osborn, C. (2004). Use of visual reaction time to assess male adolescents who molest children. *Sexual Abuse: A Journal of Research and Treatment, 16*, 255-265.

Aebi, M., Plattner, B., Steinhausen, H-C., & Bessler, C. (2011). Predicting sexual and nonsexual recidivism in a consecutive sample of juveniles convicted of sexual offences. *Sexual Abuse: Journal of Research and Treatment23*, 456-473.

Ageton, S. S. (1983). *Sexual assault among adolesents.* Lexington, MA: Lexington Books.

Andrews, D. A., & Bonta, J. (2010). Rehabilitating criminal justice policy and practice. *Psychology, Public Policy, and Law, 16*(1), 39-55.

Andrews, D. A., Bonta, J., & Hoge, R. D. (1990). Classification for effective rehabilitation: Rediscovering psychology. *Criminal Justice and Behavior, 17*, 19-52.

Aos, S., Phipps, P., Barnoski, R., & Lieb, R. (2001, May). *The comparative costs and benefits of programs to reduce crime.* Version 4.0. Document Number 01-05-1201. Olympia, WA: Washington State Institute for Public Policy.

Arnett, J. J. (2010). Emerging adulthood: The winding road from the late teens through the twenties. *Perspectives on Psychological Science, 5*(1), 89-92.

Association for the Treatment of Sexual Abusers. (2012). Adolescents who have engaged in sexually abusive behavior: Effective policies and practices. http://www.atsa.com/adolescents-engaged-in-sexually-abusive-behavior

Barbaree, H. E., & Marshall, W. L. (2006). An introduction to the juvenile sex offender: Terms, concepts, and definitions. In H. E. Barbaree & W. L. Marshall (Eds.), *The juvenile sex offender* (2nd ed., pp. 1-18). New York, NY: Guilford Press.

Becker, J. V., & Hunter, J. A. (1997). Understanding and treating child and adolescent sexual offenders. In T. H. Ollendick & R. J. Prinz (Eds.), *Advances in clinical child psychology* (Vol. 19, pp. 177-197). New York, NY: Plenum Press.

Becker, J. V., & Kaplan, M. S. (1988). The assessment of adolescent sexual offenders. In R. J. Prinz (Ed.), *Advances in behavioral assessment of children & families* (pp. 97-118). Greenwich, CT: JAI Press.

Belsky, J. (1980). Child maltreatment: An ecological integration. *American Psychologist, 35,* 320-335.

Bischof, G. P., Stith, S. M., & Whitney, M. L. (1995). Family environments of adolescent sex offenders and other juvenile delinquents. *Adolescence, 30,* 157-170.

Bischof, G. P., Stith, S. M., & Wilson, S. M. (1992). A comparison of the family systems of adolescent sexual offenders and nonsexual offending delinquents. *Family Relations, 41,* 318-323.

Blaske, D. M., Borduin, C. M., Henggeler, S. W., & Mann, B. J. (1989). Individual, family, and peer characteristics of adolescent sex offenders and assaultive offenders. *Developmental Psychology, 25,* 846-855.

Boelema, S. R., Harakeh, Z., Ormel, J., Hartman, C. A., Vollebergh, W. A. M., & van Zandvoort, M. J. E. (2014). Executive functioning shows differential maturation from early to late adolescence: Longitudinal findings from a TRAILS study. *Neuropsychology, 28*(2), 177-187.

Bonner, B. (2009). *Taking action: Support for families of adolescents with illegal sexual behavior.* Brandon, VT: Safer Society Press.

Bonnie, R. J., & Scott, E. S. (2013). The teenage brain: Adolescent brain research and the law. *Current Directions in Psychological Science, 22,* 158-161.

Borduin, C. M., Henggeler, S. W., Blaske, D. M., & Stein, R. J. (1990). Multisystemic treatment of adolescent sexual offenders. *International Journal of Offender Therapy and Comparative Criminology, 34,* 105-113.

Borduin, C. M., Schaeffer, & Heilblum, N. (2009). A randomized clinical trial of Multisystemic Therapy with juvenile sexual offenders: Effects on youth social ecology and criminal activity. *Journal of Consulting and Clinical Psychology, 77*(1), 26-37.

Borum, R., Bartel, P., & Forth, A. (2002). *Manual for the Structured Assessment of Violence Risk in Youth (SAVRY)*, consultation edition, version 1. Tampa, FL: University of South Florida.

Bourke, M. L., & Donohue, B. (1996). Assessment and treatment of juvenile sex offenders: An empirical review. *Journal of Child Sexual Abuse, 5*(1), 47-70.

Bremer, J. (2006). Protective Factors Scale: Determining the level of intervention for youth with harmful sexual behavior. In D. S. Prescott (Ed.), *Risk assessment of youth who have sexually abused* (pp. 195-221). Oklahoma City, OK: Wood 'N' Barnes.

Bronfenbrenner, U. (1979). *The ecology of human development.* Cambridge, MA: Harvard University Press.

Caldwell, M. F. (2010). Study characteristics and recidivism base rates in juvenile sex offender recidivism. *International Journal of Offender Therapy and Comparative Criminology, 54,* 197-212.

Caldwell, M. F. (2013). Accuracy of sexually violent person assessments of juveniles adjudicated for sexual offenses. *Sexual Abuse: Journal of Research and Treatment, 25,* 516-526.

Caldwell, M. F., & Dickenson, C.(2009). Sex offender registration and recidivism risk in juvenile sexual offenders. *Behavioral Science and the Law, 27*(6), 941-956.

Caldwell, M. F., McCormick, J., Umstead, D., & Van Rybroek, G. J. (2007). Evidence of treatment progress and therapeutic outcomes among adolescents with psychopathic features. *Criminal Justice and Behavior, 34,* 573-587.

Caldwell, M. F., Skeem, J., Salekin, R., & Van Rybroek, G. (2006). Treatment response of adolescent offenders with psychopathy features: A 2-year follow-up. *Criminal Justice and Behavior, 33,* 571-596.

Caldwell, M. F., Ziemke, M. H., & Vitacco, M. J. (2008). An examination of the Sex Offender Registration and Notification Act as applied to juveniles: Evaluating the ability to predict sexual recidivism. *Psychology, Public Policy, and Law, 14*(2), 89-114.

Carpentier, J., Leclerc, B., & Proulx, J. (2011). Juvenile sexual offenders: Correlates of onset, variety, and desistance of criminal behavior. *Criminal Justice and Behavior, 38,* 854-873.

Carpentier, J., & Proulx, J. (2011). Correlates of recidivism among adolescents who have sexually offended. *Sexual Abuse: Journal of Research and Treatment, 23,* 434-455.

Carpentier, M. Y., Silovsky, J. F., & Chaffin, M. (2006). Randomized trial of treatment for children with sexual behavior problems: Ten-year follow-up. *Journal of Consulting and Clinical Psychology, 74,* 482-488.

Chaffin, M. (2008). Our minds are made up—Don't confuse us with the facts: Commentary on policies concerning children with sexual behavior problems and juvenile sex offenders. *Child Maltreatment, 13,* 110-121.

Chaffin, M. (2010). The case of juvenile polygraphy as a clinical ethics dilemma. *Sexual Abuse: A Journal of Research and Treatment, 23,* 314-328.

Chaffin, M., & Bonner, B. (1998). Don't shoot, we're your children: Have we gone too far in our response to adolescent sexual abusers and children with sexual behavior problems. *Child Maltreatment, 3,* 314-316.

Chamberlain, P., Leve, L. D., & DeGarmo, D. S. (2007). Multidimensional treatment foster care for girls in the juvenile justice system: 2-year follow-up of a randomized clinical trial. *Journal of Consulting and Clinical Psychology, 75*(1), 187-193.

Chamberlain, P., & Reid, J. B. (1998). Comparison of two community alternatives to incarceration for chronic juvenile offenders. *Journal of Consulting and Clinical Psychology, 66,* 624-633.

Ciarrochi, J., Deane, F. P., Wilson, C. J., & Rickwood, D. (2002). Adolescents who need help the most are the least likely to seek it: The relationship between low emotional competence and low intention to seek help. *British Journal of Guidance & Counselling, 30,* 173-188.

Clift, R. J. W., Rajlic, G., & Gretton, H. M. (2009). Discriminative and predictive validity of the penile plethysmograph in adolescent sex offenders. *Sexual Abuse: Journal of Research and Treatment, 21,* 335-362.

Cottle, C., Lee, R., & Heilbrun, K. (2001). The prediction of criminal recidivism in juveniles: A meta-analysis. *Criminal Justice and Behavior, 28,* 367-394.

Curtis, N. M., Ronan, K. R., & Borduin, C. M. (2004). Multisystemic Treatment: A meta-analysis of outcome studies. *Journal of Family Psychology, 18,* 411-419.

Daversa, M., & Knight, R. A. (2007). A structural examination of the predictors of sexual coercion against children in adolescent sexual offenders. *Criminal Justice and Behavior, 34,* 1313-1333.

Department of Health and Human Services. (2001). *Youth violence: A report of The Surgeon General.* Rockville, MD: Department of Health and Human Services. http://www.surgeongeneral.gov/library/youthviolence/default.htm

Driemeyer, W., Yoon, D.,& Briken, P. (2011). Sexuality, antisocial behavior, aggressiveness, and victimization in juvenile sexual offenders: A literature review. *Sexual Offender Treatment, 6*(1). http://www.sexual-offender-treatment.org/95.html

Eddy, M. J., Whaley, R. B., & Chamberlain, P. (2004). The prevention of violent behavior by chronic and serious male juvenile offenders: A 2-year follow-up of a randomized clinical trial. *Journal of Family Psychology, 12*(1), 2-8.

Efta-Breitbach, J., & Freeman, K. A. (2004). Treatment of juveniles who sexually offend: An overview. *Journal of Child Sexual Abuse, 13*(3-4), 125-138.

Epperson, D. L., Ralston, C. A., Fowers, D., & Dewitt, J. (2005). *Development of the Juvenile Sexual Offense Recidivism Risk Assessment Tool-II (JSORRAT-II).* Retrieved from: http://www.psychology.iastate.edu/faculty/epperson/jsorrat-ii-download.htm

Epperson, D. L., Ralston, C. A., Fowers, D., & Dewitt, J. (2006). Development of the Juvenile Sexual Offense Recidivism Risk Assessment Tool-II (JSORRAT-II). In D. S. Prescott (Ed.), *Knowledge & practice: Challenges in the treatment and supervision of sexual abusers* (pp. 310-344). Oklahoma City, OK: Wood 'N' Barnes.

Fanniff, A. M., & Becker, J. V. (2006). Specialized assessment and treatment of adolescent sex offenders. *Aggression and Violent Behavior, 11*(3), 265-282.

Farmer, M., Beech, A. R., & Ward, T. (2012). Assessing desistance in child molesters: A qualitative analysis. *Journal of Interpersonal Violence, 27,* 930-950.

Fehrenbach, P. A., Smith, W., Monastersky, C., & Deisher, R. W. (1986). Adolescent sexual offenders: Offender and offense characteristics. *American Journal of Orthopsychiatry, 56,* 225-233.

Ferrara, M. L., & McDonald, S. (1996). *Treatment of the juvenile sex offender: Neurological and psychiatric impairments.* Northvale, NJ: J. Aronson.

Finkelhor, D. (1984). *Child sexual abuse: New theory & research.* New York, NY: The Free Press.

Finkelhor, D., Ormrod, R., Chaffin, M. (2009, December). Juveniles who commit sex offenses against minors. Retrieved from: www.ojp.usdoj.gov/ojjdp

Ford, J. D., Chapman, J., Conner, D. F., & Cruise, K. R. (2012). Complex trauma and aggression in secure juvenile justice settings. *Criminal Justice and Behavior, 39,* 694-724.

Forth, A. E., Kosson, D., & Hare, R. D. (2003). *The Hare PCL: Youth Version.* Toronto, Canada: Multi-Health Systems.

France, K. G., & Hudson, S. M. (1993). The conduct disorders and the juvenile sex offender. In H. E. Barbaree, W. L. Marshall, & S. M. Hudson (Eds.), *The juvenile sex offender* (pp. 225-234). New York, NY: Guilford Press.

Frey, C. L. (1995). *Double jeopardy: Treating juvenile victims and perpetrators for the dual disorder of sexual abuse and substance abuse.* Dubuque, IA: Islewest Publishing.

Friedrich, W. M., Lysne, M., Sim, L., & Shamos, S. (2004). Assessing sexual behavior in high-risk adolescents with the Adolescent Clinical Sexual Behavior Inventory (ACSBI). *Child Maltreatment, 9,* 239-250.

Gannon, T. A., & Cortoni, F. (2010). *Female sexual offenders: Theory, assessment and treatment.* West Sussex, UK: Wiley-Blackwell.

Graves, R., Openshaw, D. K., & Adams, G. R. (1992). Adolescent sex offenders and social skills training. *International Journal of Offender Therapy and Comparative Criminology, 36,* 139-153.

Gretton, H. M., McBride, M., Hare, R. D., O'Shaughnessy, R., & Kumka, G. (2001). Psychopathy and recidivism in adolescent sex offenders. *Criminal Justice and Behavior, 28,* 427-499.

Griffin, H. L., Beech, A., Print, B., Bradshaw, H., & Quayle, J. (2008). The development and initial testing of the AIM-2 framework to assess risk and strengths in young people who sexually offend. *Journal of Sexual Aggression, 14,* 211-225.

Hanson, R. K., Bourgon, G., Helmus, L., & Hodgson, S. (2009). The principles of effective correctional treatment also apply to sexual offenders: A meta-analysis. *Criminal Justice and Behavior, 36,* 865-891.

Hanson, R. K., & Bussière, M. T. (1998). Predicting relapse: A meta-analysis of sexual offender recidivism studies. *Journal of Consulting and Clinical Psychology, 66,* 348-362.

Hanson, R. K., Gordon, A., Harris, A. J. R., Marques, J. K., Murphy, W., Quinsey, V. L., & Seto, M. C. (2002). First report of the collaborative outcome data project on the effectiveness of psychological treatment for sex offenders. *Sexual Abuse: A Journal of Research and Treatment, 14*, 169-194.

Hanson, R. K., & Harris, A. J. R. (2000). Where should we intervene?: Dynamic predictors of sexual assault recidivism. *Criminal Justice and Behavior, 27*(1), 6-35.

Hanson, R. K., & Morton-Bourgon, K. (2005). The characteristics of persistent sexual offenders: A meta-analysis of recidivism studies. *Journal of Consulting and Clinical Psychology, 73*(6), 1154-1163.

Hare, R. D., Harpur, T. J., Hakstian, A. R., Forth, A. E., Hart, S. D., & Newman, J. P. (1990). The Revised Psychopathy Checklist: Reliability and factor structure. *Psychological Assessment, 2,* 338-341.

Hawkins, J. D., Herrenkohl, T. I., Farrington, D. P., Brewer, D., Catalano, R. F., Harachi, T. W., & Cothern, L. (1998*).* A review of predictors of youth violence. In R. Loeber & D. P. Farrington (Eds.), *Serious & violent juvenile offender: Risk factors and successful interventions* (pp. 106-146). Thousand Oaks, CA: Sage Publications.

Hawkins, J. D., Herrenkohl, T. I., Farrington, D. P., Brewer, D. D., Catalano, R. F., Harachi, T. W., & Cothern, L. (2000). Predictors of youth violence. *OJJDP: Juvenile Justice Bulletin,* Washington, DC.

Hecker, J. E. (2014). Baby with the bath water: A response to Fanniff and Letourneau. *Sexual Abuse: A Journal of Research and Treatment,* published online 28 February 2014.

Heilbrun, K., Lee, R. J., & Cottle, C. C. (2005). Risk factors and intervention outcomes: Meta-analyses of juvenile offending. In K. Heilbrun, N. E. S. Goldstein, & R. E. Redding, *Juvenile delinquency: Prevention, assessment, & interventio*n (pp. 111-133). New York, NY: Oxford University Press.

Helmus, L., Hanson, R. K., Babchishin, K. M., & Mann, R. E. (2013). Attitudes supportive of sexual offending predict recidivism: A meta-analysis. *Trauma, Violence, & Abuse, 14*(1), 34-53.

Henggeler, S. W., Letourneau, E. J., Chapman, J. E., Borduin, C. M., Schewe, P. A., & McCart, M. R. (2009). Mediators of change for multisystemic therapy with juvenile sexual offenders. *Journal of Consulting and Clinical Psychology, 77*(3), 451-462.

Henggeler, S. W., Melton, G. B., Brondino, M. J., Scherer, D. G., & Hanley, J. H. (1997). Multisystemic Therapy with violent and chronic juvenile offenders and their families: The role of treatment fidelity in successful dissemination. *Journal of Consulting and Clinical Psychology, 65,* 821-833.

Henggeler, S. W., Schoenwald, S. K., Borduin, C. M., Rowland, M. D., & Cunningham, P. B. (1998). *Multisystemic treatment of antisocial behavior in children and adolescents.* New York, NY: Guilford Press.

Herman-Giddens, M. E., Wang, L., & Koch G. (2001). Secondary sexual characteristics in boys: Estimates from the National Health and Nutrition Examination Survey III, 1988-1994. *Archives of Pediatric and Adolescent Medicine, 155,* 1022-1028.

Herrenkohl, T. I., McMorris, B. J., Catalono, R. F., Abbott, R. D., Hemphill, S. A., & Toumbourou, J. W. (2007). Risk factors for violence and relational aggression in adolescence. *Journal of Interpersonal Violence, 2,* 386-405.

Hessler, D. M., & Katz, L. F. (2010). Brief report: Associations between emotional competence and adolescent risky behavior. *Journal of Adolescence, 33,* 241-246.

Howell, A. J., Reddon, J. R., & Enns, R. A. (1997). Immediate antecedents to adolescents' offenses. *Journal of Clinical Psychology, 53,* 355-360.

Hubbard, D. J., & Matthews, B. (2008). Reconciling the differences between the "gender-responsive" and the "what works" literatures to improve services for girls. *Crime & Delinquency, 54*(2), 225-258.

Hunter, J. A. (2006). Understanding diversity in juvenile sexual offenders: Implications for assessment, treatment, and legal management. In R. E. Longo & D. S. Prescott (Eds.), *Current perspectives: Working with sexually aggressive youth and youth with sexual behavior problems* (pp. 63-77). Holyoke, MA: NEARI Press.

Hunter, J. A., Jr., & Becker, J. V. (1994). The role of deviant sexual arousal in juvenile sexual offending: Etiology, evaluation, and treatment. *Criminal Justice and Behavior, 21*(1), 132-149.

Hunter, J. A., Jr., & Figueredo, A. J. (1999). Factors associated with treatment compliance in a population of juvenile sexual offenders. *Sexual Abuse: A Journal of Research and Treatment, 11*(1), 49-67.

Hunter, J. A., Figueredo, A. J., & Malamuth, N. M. (2010). Developmental pathways into social and sexual deviance. *Journal of Family Violence, 25,* 141-148.

Hunter, J. A., Figueredo, A. J., Malamuth, N. M., & Becker, J. V. (2004). Developmental pathways in youth sexual aggression and delinquency: Risk factors and mediators. *Journal of Family Violence, 19*(4), 233-242.

Hyde, J. S., & DeLamater, J. D. (1997). *Understanding human sexuality* (6th ed.). New York, NY: McGraw-Hill Book Company.

Jenkins, A. (2006). Discovering integrity: Working with shame without shaming young people who have abused. In R. E. Longo & D. S. Prescott (Eds.), *Current perspectives: Working with sexually aggressive youth and youth with sexual behavior problems* (pp. 63-77). Holyoke, MA: NEARI Press.

Kahn, T. J., & Chambers, H. J. (1991). Assessing reoffense risk with juvenile sexual offenders. *Child Welfare, LXX,* 333-345.

Kendall, P., & Braswell, L. (1993) *Cognitive-behavioural therapy for impulsive children* (2nd ed.). New York, NY: Guilford Press.

Kenny, D. T., Keogh, T., & Seidler, K. (2001). Predictors of recidivism in Australian juvenile sex offenders: Implications for treatment. *Sexual Abuse: Journal of Research and Treatment, 13,* 131-148.

Kerr, D. C. R., Leve, L. D., & Chamberlain, P. (2009). Pregnancy rates among juvenile justice girls in two randomized controlled trials of multidimensional treatment foster care. *Journal of Consulting and Clinical Psychology, 77,* 588-593.

Kimball, L., & Guarino-Ghezzi, S. (1996). *Sex offender treatment: An assessment of sex offender treatment within the Massachusetts Department of Youth Services* (Juvenile Justice Series Report No. 10). Boston, MA: Northeastern University, Privatized Research Management Initiative.

Kingston, D. A., Fedoroff, P., Firestone, P., Curry, S., & Bradford, J. M. (2008). Pornography use and sexual aggression: The impact of frequency and type of pornography use on recidivism among sexual offenders. *Aggressive Behavior, 34,* 341-351.

Knight, R. A., & Guay, J.-P. (2006). The role of psychopathy in sexual coercion against women. In C. J. Christopher (Ed.), *Handbook of psychopathy* (pp. 512-532). New York, NY: Guilford Press.

Knight, R. A., & Prentky, R. A. (1993). Exploring characteristics for classifying juvenile sex offenders. In H. E. Barbaree, W. L. Marshall, & S. M. Hudson (Eds.), *The juvenile sex offender* (pp. 45-83). New York, NY: Guilford Press.

Knight, R. A., Ronis, S. T., & Zakireh, B. (2009). Bootstrapping persistence risk indicators for juveniles who sexually offend. *Behavioral Sciences and the Law, 27*, 878-909.

Knight, R. A., & Sims-Knight, J. E. (2004). Testing an etiological model for male juvenile sexual offending against females. *Journal of Child Sexual Abuse, 13*(3-4), 33-55.

Kraemer, B. D., Salisbury, S. B., & Spielman, C. R. (1998). Pretreatment variables associated with treatment failure in a residential juvenile sex-offender program. *Criminal Justice and Behavior, 25*, 190-202.

Lab, S., Shields, G., & Schondel, C. (1993). Research note: An evaluation of juvenile sexual offender treatment. *Crime & Delinquency, 39*, 543-553.

Lambie, I., & McCarthy, J. (2004). Interviewing strategies with sexually abusive youth. *Journal of Child Sexual Abuse: Research, Treatment, & Program Innovations for Victims, Survivors, & Offenders, 13*(3-4), 107-123.

Långström, N., & Grann, M. (2000). Risk for criminal recidivism among young sex offenders. *Journal of Interpersonal Violence, 15*, 855-871.

Langton, C. M., Barbaree, H. E., Harkins, L., Arenovich, T., McNamee, J., Peacock, E. J., et al. (2008). Denial and minimization among sexual offenders: Posttreatment presentation and association with sexual recidivism. *Criminal Justice and Behavior, 35*(1), 69-98.

Leschied, A. W., & Cunningham, A. (2002). Seeking effective interventions for serious young offenders: Interim results of a four-year randomized study of Multisystemic Therapy in Ontario, Canada. http://www.lfcc.on.ca/seeking.html

Letourneau, E. J., & Armstrong, K. S. (2008). Recidivism rates for registered and nonregistered juvenile sexual offenders. *Sexual Abuse: Journal of Research and Treatment, 20*, 393-408.

Letourneau, E. J., Armstrong, K. S., Bandyopadhyay, D., & Sinha, D. (2013). Sex offender registration and notification policy increases juvenile plea bargains. *Sexual Abuse: Journal of Research and Treatment, 25*, 189-207.

Letourneau, E. J., Henggeler, S. W., Borduin, C. M., Schewe, P. A., McCart, M. R., Chapman, J. E., & Saldana, L. (2009). Multisystemic Therapy for juvenile sexual offenders: 1-year results from a randomized effectiveness trial. *Journal of Family Psychology, 23*, 89-102.

Lindsay, W. R. (2005). Model underpinning treatment for sex offenders with mild intellectual disability: Current theories of sex offending. *Mental Retardation, 43*, 428–441.

Lipsey, M. W. (1995). What do we learn from 400 research studies on the effectiveness of treatment with juvenile delinquents? In J. McGuire (Ed.). *What works? Reducing reoffending* (pp. 63-78). New York, NY: John Wiley.

Lipsey, M. W. (1999). Can intervention rehabilitate serious delinquents? *The Annals of the American Academy of Political and Social Science, 564*, 142-166.

Lipsey, M. W. (2009). The primary factors that characterize effective interventions with juvenile offenders: A meta-analytic overview. *Victims & Offenders, 4,* 124-147.

Lipsey, M. W., & Derzon, J. H. (1998). Predictors of violence and serious delinquency in adolescence and serious adulthood: A synthesis of longitudinal research. In R. Loeber & D. P. Farrington (Eds.), *Serious & violent juvenile offender: Risk factors and successful interventions* (pp. 86-105). Thousand Oaks, CA: Sage Publications.

Littell, J., Popa M., & Forsythe, B. (2005). Multisystemic Therapy for social, emotional, and behavioral problems in youth aged 10-17. *Campbell Systematic Reviews, 1.*

Malamuth, N. M., & Brown, L. M. (1994). Sexually aggressive men's perceptions of women's communications: Testing three explanations. *Journal of Personality and Social Psychology, 67,* 699-712.

Malamuth, N. M., Linz, D., Heavey, C. L., Barnes, G., & Acker, M. (1995). Using the confluence model of sexual aggression to predict men's conflict with women: A 10-year follow-up study. *Journal of Personality and Social Psychology, 69,* 353-369.

Marlowe, D. B., Festinger, D. S., Lee, P. A., Dugosh, K. L., & Benasutti, K. M. (2006). Matching judicial supervision to clients' risk status in drug court. *Crime & Delinquency, 52*(1), 52-76.

Marohn, R. C. (1992). Management of the assaultive adolescent. *Hospital and Community Psychiatry, 43,* 622-624.

Marques, J. K., Wiederanders, M., Day, D. M., Nelson, C., & van Ommeren, A. (2005). Effects of a relapse prevention program on sexual recidivism: Final results from California's Sex Offender Treatment and Evaluation Project (SOTEP). *Sexual Abuse: A Journal of Research and Treatment, 7,* 79-107.

Marshall, W. L. (2005). Therapist style in sexual offender treatment: Influence on indices of change. *Sexual Abuse: A Journal of Research and Treatment, 17,* 109-116.

Marshall, W. L., Thornton, D., Marshall, L. E., Fernandez, Y. M., & Mann, R. E. (2001). Treatment of sexual offenders who are in categorical denial: A pilot project. *Sexual Abuse: A Journal of Research and Treatment, 13,* 205-215.

McCann, K., & Lussier, P. (2008). Antisociality, sexual deviance, and sexual reoffending in juvenile sex offenders: A meta-analytical investigation. *Youth Violence and Juvenile Justice, 6,* 363-385.

McGowan, M. R., Horn, R. A., & Mellott, R. N. (2011), The predictive validity of the Structured Assessment of Violence Risk in Youth in secondary educational settings. *Psychological Assessment, 23*(2), 478-486.

McGrath, R. J., Cumming, G. F., Burchard, B. L., Zeoli, S., & Ellerby, L. (2010). *Current practices and trends in sexual abuser management: The Safer Society 2009 nationwide survey.* Brandon, VT: Safer Society Press.

McPhail, I. V., Hermann, C. A., & Nunes, K. L. (2013). Emotional congruence with children and sexual offending against children: A meta-analytic review. *Journal of Consulting and Clinical Psychology, 81,* 737-749.

Melton, G. B., Petrila, J., Poythress, N. G., & Slobogin, C. (2007). *Psychological Evaluations for the Courts: A handbook for mental health professionals and lawyers* (3rd ed.). New York, NY: Guilford Press.

Meyers, J. R., & Schmidt, R. (2008). Predictive validity of the Structured Assessment for Violence Risk in Youth (SAVRY). *Criminal Justice and Behavior, 35*(3), 344-355.

Milloy, C. D. (1994). *A comparative study of juvenile sex offenders and non-sex offenders.* Washington State Institute for Public Policy, Olympia, WA.

Miner, M. H., & Crimmins, C. L. S. (1995). Adolescent sex offenders: Issues of etiology and risk factors. In B. K. Schwartz, & H. K. Cellini (Eds.), *The sex offender: Vol. 1. Corrections, treatment and legal practice* (pp. 9.1-9.15). Kingston, NJ: Civic Research Institute.

Miner, M. H., Robinson, B., Knight, R., Berg, D., Romine, R. S., & Netland, J. (2010). Understanding sexual perpetration against children: Effects of attachment style, interpersonal involvement, and hypersexuality. *Sexual Abuse: A Journal of Research and Treatment, 2*(1), 58-77.

Miner, M. H., Siekert, G. P., & Ackland, M. A. (1997). *Evaluation: Juvenile sex offender treatment program, Minnesota Correctional Facility—Sauk Centre* (Final report—Biennium 1995-1997). Minneapolis, MN: University of Minnesota, Department of Family Practice and Community Health, Program in Human Sexuality.

Modecki, K. L. (2008). Addressing gaps in the maturity of judgment literature: Age differences and delinquency. *Law and Human Behavior, 32,* 78-91.

Moffitt, T. (1993). Adolescence-limited and life-course-persistent antisocial behavior: A developmental taxonomy. *Psychological Review, 100,* 674-701.

Monahan, K. C., Steinberg, L., & Cauffman, E. (2009). Affiliation with antisocial peers, susceptibility to peer influence, and desistance from antisocial behavior during the transition to adulthood. *Developmental Psychology, 45,* 1520-1530.

Morris, R. E., Anderson, M. M., & Knox, G. W. (2002). Incarcerated adolescents' experiences as perpetrators of sexual assault. *Archives of Pediatrics & Adolescent Medicine, 156,* 831-835.

Multisystemic Therapy Services, Inc. (n.d.). Retrieved from http://mstservices.com/target-populations/problem-sexual-behavior. Accessed on July 14, 2014.

New, M. J. C., Stevenson, J., & Skuse, D. (1999). Characteristics of mothers of boys who sexually abuse. *Child Maltreatment, 4,* 21-31.

Nichols, H. R., & Molinder, I. (1984). *Multiphasic Sex Inventory manual.* Fircrest, WA: Nichols & Molinder Assessment Inc.

Nisbet, I. A., Wilson, P. H., & Smallbone, S. W. (2004). A prospective longitudinal study of sexual recidivism among adolescent sex offenders. *Sexual Abuse: A Journal of Research and Treatment, 16,* 223-234.

Nunes, K. L., Hanson, R. K., Firestone, P., Moulden, H. M., Greenberg, D. M., & Bradford, J. M. (2007). Denial predicts recidivism for some sexual offenders. *Sexual Abuse: A Journal of Research and Treatment, 19,* 91-105.

O'Brien, M. & Bera, W. (1986). Adolescent sexual offenders: A descriptive typology. *A Newsletter of the National Family Life Education Network, 1,* 1-5.

Ogden, T., & Hagen, K. A. (2006). Multisystemic treatment of serious behaviour problems in youth: Sustainability of effectiveness two years after intake. *Child and Adolescent Mental Health, 11,* 142-149.

Ogden, T., & Hagen, K. A. (2009). What works for whom? Gender differences in intake characteristics and treatment outcomes following Multisystemic Therapy. *Journal of Adolescence, 3,* 1425-1435.

O'Reilly, G. O., Morrison, T., Sheerin, D., & Carr, A. (2001). A group-based module for adolescents to improve motivation to change sexually abusive behavior. *Child Abuse Review, 10,* 150-169.

Page, J., & Murphy, W. D. (2007). *Manual for structured group treatment with adolescent sex offenders.* Brandon, VT: Safer Society Press.

Parks, G. A., & Bard, D. E. (2006). Risk factors for adolescent sex offender recidivism: Evaluation of predictive factors and comparison of three groups based upon victim type. *Sexual Abuse: Journal of Research and Treatment, 18,* 319-342.

Pealer, J. A., & Latessa, E. J. (2004, December). Applying the principles of effective interventions to juvenile corrections. *Corrections Today,* pp. 26-29.

Powers-Sawyer, A., & Miner, M. (2009). Actuarial prediction of juvenile recidivism: The static variables of the Juvenile Sex Offender Assessment Protocol-II (J-SOAP-II). *Sexual Offender Treatment, 4*(2), 1-11.

Prentky, R. A., Janus, E., Barbaree, H., Schwartz, B. K., & Kafka, M. P. (2006). Sexually violent predators in the courtroom: Science on trial. *Psychology, Public Policy, and Law, 12*(4), 357-393.

Prentky, R. A., & Righthand, S. (2003). *Juvenile Sex Offender Assessment Protocol: Manual.* Washington, DC: Office of Juvenile Justice and Delinquency Prevention.

Prochaska, J. O., DiClemente, C. C., & Norcross, J. C. (1992). In search of how people change: Applications to addictive behaviors. *American Psychologist, 47,* 1102-1114.

Proulx, J., & Carpentier, J. (2011). Correlates of recidivism among adolescents who have sexually offended. *Sexual Abuse: Journal of Research and Treatment, 23(4),* 434-455.

Proulx, J., McKibben, A., & Lusignan, R. (1996). Relationships between affective components and sexual behaviors in sexual aggressors. *Sexual Abuse: Journal of Research and Treatment, 8,* 279-289.

Pullman, L., & Seto, M. C. (2012). Assessment and treatment of adolescent sexual offenders: Implications of recent research on generalist versus specialist explanations. *Child Abuse & Neglect, 36,* 203-209.

Quinsey, V., Rice, M., & Harris, G. (1995). Actuarial prediction of sexual recidivism. *Journal of Interpersonal Violence, 10,* 85-105.

Quinsey, V. L., Skilling, T. A., Lalumière, M. L., & Craig, W. M. (2004) Evolutionary psychology. In *Juvenile delinquency: Understanding the origins of individual differences.* Washington DC: American Psychological Association.

Rajlic, G., & Gretton, H. M. (2010). An examination of two sexual recidivism risk measures in adolescent offenders: The moderating effect of offender type. *Criminal Justice and Behavior, 37,* 1066-1085.

Ralston, C. A., & Epperson, D. L. (2013). Predictive validity of adult risk assessment tools with juveniles who offended sexually. *Psychological Assessment, 25,* 905-916.

Rasmussen, L. A. (1999). Factors related to recidivism among juvenile sex offenders. *Sexual Abuse: A Journal of Research and Treatment, 11*(1), 69-85.

Reid, J. B. (1993). Prevention of conduct disorder before and after school entry: Relating interventions to developmental psychopathology. *Developmental and Psychopathology, 5,* 311-319.

Reitzel, L. R., & Carbonell, J. L. (2006). The effectiveness of sexual offender treatment for juveniles as measured by recidivism: A meta-analysis. *Sexual Abuse: Journal of Research and Treatment, 18,* 401-421.

Rich, P. (2003). *Understanding, assessing, and rehabilitating juvenile sexual offenders.* Hoboken, NJ: John Wiley & Sons.

Rich, P. (2009). *Juvenile Sexual Offenders: A Comprehensive Guide to Risk Evaluation.* Hoboken, NJ: John Wiley & Sons.

Rich, P. (2011). *Understanding, Assessing, and Rehabilitating Juvenile Sexual Offenders* (2nd ed.). Hoboken, NJ: John Wiley & Sons.

Righthand, S., Prentky, R., Knight, R., Carpenter, E., Hecker, J. E., & Nangle, D. (2005). Factor structure and validation of the Juvenile Sex Offender Assessment Protocol (J–SOAP). *Sex Abuse: Journal of Research and Treatment, 17*(1), 13-30.

Righthand, S., & Welch, C. (2001). *Youths who have sexually offended: A review of the professional literature.* Washington, DC: Office of Juvenile Justice and Delinquency Prevention.

Righthand, S., & Welch, C. (2004). Characteristics of youth who sexually offend. *Journal of Child Sexual Abuse, 13*(3-4), 15-32.

Rogstad, J. E., & Rogers, R. (2008). Gender differences in contributions of emotion to psychopathy and antisocial personality disorder. *Clinical Psychological Review, 28,* 1472-1484.

Ronis, S. T., & Borduin, C. M. (2007). Individual, family, peer, and academic characteristics of male juvenile sexual offenders. *Journal of Abnormal Child Psychology, 35,* 153-163.

Ryan, E. P., Hunter, J. A., & Murrie, D. C. (2012) *Juvenile sex offenders: A guide to evaluation and treatment for mental health professionals.* New York, NY: Oxford University Press.

Ryan, G., Miyoshi, T., Metzner, J. L., Krugman, R. D., & Fryer, G. E. (1996). Trends in a national sample of sexually abusive youths. *Journal of the American Academy of Child and Adolescent Psychiatry, 35,* 17-25.

Sabina, C., Wolak, J., & Finkelhor, D. (2008). The nature and dynamics of Internet pornography exposure for youth. *CyberPsychology & Behavior, 11,* 691-693.

Sampson, R. J., & Laub, J. H. (2003). *Shared beginnings, divergent lives: Delinquent boys to age 70.* Cambridge, MA: Harvard University Press.

Sawyer, A. M., & Borduin, C. M. (2011). Effects of Multisystemic Therapy through midlife: A 21.9-year follow-up to a randomized clinical trial with serious and violent juvenile offenders. *Journal of Consulting and Clinical Psychology, 79,* 643-652.

Schmucker, M., & Lösel, F. (2008). Does sexual offender treatment work? A systematic review of outcome evaluations. *Psicothema, 20*(1), 10-19.

Schram, D. D., Milloy, C. D., & Rowe, W. E. (1991*). Juvenile sex offenders: A follow-up study of reoffense behavior.* Washington State Institute for Public Policy, Olympia, WA.

Seabloom, W., Seabloom, M. E., Seabloom, E., Barron, R. R., & Hendrickson, S. (2003). A 14- to 24-year longitudinal study of a comprehensive sexual health model treatment program for adolescent sex offenders: Predictors of successful completion and subsequent criminal recidivism. *International Journal of Offender Therapy and Comparative Criminology, 47,* 468-481.

Seager, J. A., Jellicoe, D., & Dhaliwal, G. K. (2004). Refusers, dropouts, and completers: Measuring sex offender treatment efficacy. *International Journal of Offender Therapy and Comparative Criminology, 48*(5), 600-612.

Seto, M. C. (2008). *Pedophilia and sexual offending against children: Theory, assessment, and intervention.* Washington, DC: American Psychological Association.

Seto, M. C. (2013). *Internet sex offenders.* Washington, DC: American Psychological Association.

Seto, M. C., & Barbaree, H. E. (1995). The role of alcohol in sexual aggression. *Clinical Psychology Review, 15,* 545-566.

Seto, M. C., & Barbaree, H. E. (1999). Psychopathy, treatment behavior, and sex offender recidivism. *Journal of Interpersonal Violence, 14,* 1235-1248.

Seto, M. C., Harris, G. T., Rice, M. E., & Barbaree, H. E. (2004). The Screening Scale for Pedophilic Interests predicts recidivism among adult sex offenders with child victims. *Archives of Sexual Behavior, 33,* 455-466.

Seto, M. C., & Lalumière, M. L. (2010). What is so special about male adolescent sexual offending? A review and test of explanations using meta-analysis. *Psychological Bulletin, 136,* 526-575.

Seto, M. C., Lalumière, M. L., & Blanchard, R. (2000). The discriminative validity of a phallometric test for pedophilic interests among adolescent sex offenders against children. *Psychological Assessment, 12,* 319-327.

Seto, M. C., Marques, J. K., Harris, G. T., Chaffin, M., Lalumière, M. L., Miner, M. H., Berliner, L., Rice, M. E., Lieb, R., & Quinsey, V. L. (2008). Good science and progress in sex offender treatment are intertwined: A response to Marshall and Marshall (2007). *Sexual Abuse: A Journal of Research and Treatment, 20,* 247-255.

Seto, M. C., Murphy, W. D., Page, J., & Ennis, L. (2003). Detecting anomalous sexual interests among juvenile sex offenders. In R. A. Prentky, E. S. Janus, & M. C. Seto (Eds.), *Annals of the New York Academy of Sciences, Vol. 989: Understanding and Managing Sexually Coercive Behavior* (pp. 118-130). New York, NY: New York Academy of Sciences.

Smith, H., & Israel, E. (1987). Sibling incest: A study of dynamics of 25 cases. *Child Abuse & Neglect, 11,* 101-108.

Smith, W. R., & Monastersky, C. (1986). Assessing juvenile sexual offenders' risk for reoffending. *Criminal Justice and Behavior, 13,* 115-140.

Spice, A., Viljoen, J. L., Latzman, N. E., Scalora, M. J., & Ullman, D. (2013). Risk and protective factors for recidivism among juveniles who have offended sexually. *Sexual Abuse: Journal of Research and Treatment, 25,* 347-369.

St. Amand, A. S., Bard, D. E., & Silovsky, J. F. (2008). Meta-analysis of treatment for child sexual behavior problems: Practice elements and outcomes. *Child Maltreatment, 13*(2), 145-166.

Steinberg, L. (2007). Risk-taking in adolescence: New perspectives from brain and behavioral science. *Current Directions in Psychological Science, 16*(2), 55-59.

Steinberg, L., & Scott, E. (2003). Less guilty by reason of adolescence: Developmental immaturity, diminished responsibility and the juvenile death penalty. *American Psychologist, 58,* 1009-1018.

Stevenson, H. C., Castillo, E., & Sefarbi, R. (1989). Treatment of denial in adolescent sex offenders and their families. *Journal of Offender Counseling, Services & Rehabilitation, 14,* 37-50.

Tangney, J. P., Stuewig, J., & Martinez, A. G. (2014). Two faces of shame: The roles of shame and guilt in predicting recidivism. *Psychological Science, 25,* 799-805.

Thoder, V. J., & Cautilli, J. D. (2011). An independent evaluation of mode deactivation therapy for juvenile offenders. *International Journal of Behavioral Consultation and Therapy, 7*(1), 41-46.

Thomas, J. (1997). The family in treatment. In G. Ryan & S. Lane (Eds.), *Juvenile sexual offending: Causes, consequences, and correction* (pp. 360-403). San Francisco, CA: Jossey-Bass Publishers.

Thomas, J. D., & Viar, C. W. (2005). Family reunification in cases of sibling incest. In M. C. Calder (Ed.), *Children and young people who sexually abuse: New theory, research and practice developments* (pp. 354-371). Dorset, UK: Russell House Publishing.

Thornton, J., Stevens, G., Grant, J., Indermaur, D., Charmette, C., & Halse, A. (2008). Intrafamilial adolescent sex offenders: Family functioning and treatment. *Journal of Family Studies, 14*(2-3), 362-375.

Timms, S., & Goreczny, A. J. (2002). Adolescent sex offenders with mental retardation: Literature review and assessment considerations. *Aggression and Violent Behavior, 7*(1), 1-19.

van der Put, C. E., Stams, G. J. J. M., Hoeve, M., Dekovic, M., Spanjaard, H. J. M., van der Laan, P. H., & Barnoski, R. P. (2012). Changes in the relative importance of dynamic risk factors for recidivism during adolescence. *International Journal of Offender Therapy and Comparative Criminology, 56,* 296-316.

van der Put, C. E., van Vugt, E. S., Stams, G. J. J. M., Deković, M., & van der Laan, P. H. (2013). Differences in the prevalence and impact of risk factors for general recidivism between different types of juveniles who have committed sexual offenses (JSOs) and juveniles who have committed nonsexual offenses (NSOs). *Sexual Abuse: A Journal of Research and Treatment, 25*(1), 41-68.

van Wijk, A., Loeber, R., Vermeiren, R., Pardini, D., Bullens, R., & Doreleijers, T. (2005). Violent juvenile sex offenders compared with violent juvenile nonsex offenders: Explorative findings from the Pittsburgh Youth Study. *Sexual Abuse: A Journal of Research and Treatment, 17,* 333-352.

Vega, V. & Malamuth, N. M. (2007). Predicting sexual aggression: The role of pornography in the context of general and specific risk factors. *Aggressive Behavior, 33,* 104-117.

Viljoen, J. L., Mordell, S., & Beneteau, J. L. (2012, February 20). Prediction of adolescent sexual reoffending: A meta-analysis of the J-SOAP-II, ERASOR, J-SORRAT-II, and Static-99. *Law and Human Behavior, 36*(5), 423-438.

Viljoen, J. L., Scalora, M., Cuadra, L., Bader, S., Chavez, V., Ullman, D., & Lawrence, L. (2008). Assessing risk of violence in adolescents who have sexually offended: A comparison of the J-SOAP-II, J-SORRAT-II, and SAVRY. *Criminal Justice and Behavior, 35*(1), 5-23.

Vincent, G. M., Chapman, J., & Cook, N. E. (2011). Risk-needs assessment in juvenile justice: Predictive validity of the SAVRY, racial differences, and the contribution of needs factors. *Criminal Justice and Behavior, 38*(1), 42-62.

Wagner, D. V., Borduin, C. M., Kanne, S. M., Mazurek, M. O., Farmer, J. E., & Brown, R. M. (in press). Multisystemic Therapy for disruptive behavior problems in youths with autism spectrum disorders: A progress report. *Journal of Marital and Family Therapy.*

Waite, D., Keller, A., McGarvey, E. L., Wieckowski, E., Pinkerton, R., & Brown, G. L. (2005). Juvenile sex offender re-arrest rates for sexual, violent nonsexual and property crimes: A 10-year follow-up. *Sexual Abuse: Journal of Research and Treatment, 17,* 313-331.

Walker, D. F., McGovern, S. K., Poey, E. L., & Otis, K. E. (2003). Treatment effectiveness for male adolescent sexual offenders: A meta-analysis and review. *Journal of Child Sexual Abuse, 13*(3/4), 281-294.

Walker, D. F., McGovern, S. K., Poey, E. L., & Otis, K. E. (2004). Treatment effectiveness for male adolescent sexual offenders: A meta-analysis and review. *Journal of Child Sexual Abuse: Research, Treatment, & Program Innovations for Victims, Survivors, & Offenders, 13,* 281-293.

Ward, T., Hudson, S. M., Marshall, W. L., & Siegert, R. (1995). Attachment style and intimacy deficits in sexual offenders: A theoretical framework. *Sexual Abuse: A Journal of Research and Treatment, 7,* 317-335.

Way, I., & Urbaniak, D. (2008). Delinquent histories of adolescents adjudicated for criminal sexual conduct. *Journal of Interpersonal Violence, 23*(9), 1197-1212.

Werner, E. E. (1993). Risk, resilience, and recovery: Perspectives from the Kauai Longitudinal Study. *Development and Psychopathology, 5,* 503-515.

Westling, E., Andrews, J. A., & Peterson, M. (2012). Gender differences in pubertal timing, social competence, and cigarette use: A test of the early maturation hypothesis. *Journal of Adolescent Health, 51*(2), 150-155.

Wiebush, R. G. (1996). *Juvenile sex offenders: Characteristics, system response, and recidivism.* Final report. Oakland, CA: National Council on Crime and Delinquency.

Worling, J. R. (2002). Assessing risk of sexual assault recidivism with adolescent sexual offenders. In M. C. Calder (Ed.), *Young people who sexually abuse: Building the evidence base for your practice* (pp. 365-375). Lyme Regis, UK: Russell House Publishing.

Worling, J. R. (2012). The assessment and treatment of deviant sexual arousal with adolescents who have offended sexually. *Journal of Sexual Aggression 18*(1), 36-63.

Worling, J. R. (2013). Desistence for Adolescents who Sexually Harm (DASH-13). http://www.erasor.org/new-protective-factors.html

Worling, J. R., Bookalam, D., & Litteljohn, A. (2012). Prospective validity of the Estimate of Risk of Adolescent Sexual Offense Recidivism (ERASOR). *Sexual Abuse: A Journal of Research and Treatment, 24,* 203-223.

Worling, J. R., & Curwen, T. (2000). Adolescent sexual offender recidivism: Success of specialized treatment and implications for risk prediction. *Child Abuse & Neglect, 24,* 965-982.

Worling, J. R., & Curwen, T. (2001). *The ERASOR: Estimate of Risk of Adolescent Sexual Recidivism (Version 2.0).* Toronto, Canada: Safe-T Program, Thistletown Regional Centre.

Worling, J. R., & Långström, N. (2003). Assessment of criminal recidivism risk with adolescents who have offended sexually: A review. *Trauma, Violence, & Abuse, 4*(4), 341-362.

Worling, J. R., & Långström, N. (2006). Risk of sexual recidivism in adolescents who offend sexually: Correlates and assessment. In H. E. Barbaree & W. L. Marshall (Eds.), *The juvenile sex offender* (2nd ed., pp. 219-247). New York, NY: Guilford Press.

Worling, J. R., & Langton, C. M. (2012). Assessment and treatment of adolescents who sexually offend: Clinical issues and implications for secure settings. *Criminal Justice and Behavior, 39*(6), 814-841.

Worling, J. R., Litteljohn, A., & Bookalam, D. (2010). 20-year prospective follow-up study of specialized treatment for adolescents who offended sexually. *Behavioral Sciences and the Law, 28,* 46-57.

Zahn, M. A., Day, J. C., Mihalic, S. F., & Tichavsky, L. (2009). Determining what works for girls in the juvenile justice system. A summary of evaluation evidence. *Crime & Delinquency, 55,* 266-293.

Zakireh, B., Ronis, S. T., & Knight, R. A. (2008). Individual beliefs, attitudes, and victimization histories of male juvenile sexual offenders. *Sexual Abuse: A Journal of Research and Treatment, 20,* 323-351.

Zimring, F. E. (2003). *The contradictions of American capital punishment.* New York, NY: Oxford University Press.

Zimring, F. E. (2004). *An American travesty: Legal responses to adolescent sexual offending.* Chicago, IL: University of Chicago Press.